WRITER'S BLOCK
AND
HOW TO USE IT

WRITER'S BLOCK

AND
HOW TO USE IT

Victoria Nelson

Cincinnati, Ohio

Library of Congress Cataloging in Publication Data

Nelson, Victoria, 1945—
    Writer's block and how to use it.

    Includes bibliographical references and index.
    1. Writer's block.   I. Title.
PN171.W74N44   1985   808' 001'9   84-29148
ISBN 0-89879-168-5

Book design by Christine Aulicino

Permissions
Acknowledgments

To the ALN fellowship that made
this book possible

CONTENTS

June 7. Bad. Wrote nothing today. Tomorrow no time.
                                        —Franz Kafka, *Diaries*

PREFACE

Serious writers, as well as anyone who has ever taken pen to hand—and then stopped—may see their own experiences reflected in the tales of woe and triumph this book records. Writer's block is, truly, the great leveler.

My approach to creative blocks draws from many precepts of the humanistic psychology movement and its ideological forebears. Perceptive readers may further note that the characteristic "I-you" polarity of "self"-help books ("I will help *you*") is almost always a projection of a dialogue conducted within the mind of the author himself—in terms of the self being helped, the ultimate Gestalt encounter. The present case is no exception. Armed with this knowledge, you, my reader, may thus be able to reap the benefits of the lessons that the original "you," myself, took so very long to learn.

The following readers deserve my thanks and gratitude for their comments and advice on the work in progress: Betsy Davids, Irving Halperin, Herbert Harari, Carolyn Kizer, Zachary Leader, Mildred Nelson, David Scalise, Lani Steele, and Ceil Sinnex. Margaret Miner and Howard I. Wells of Writer's Digest Books contributed sophisticated editorial guidance. I would also like to thank the California College of Arts and Crafts for providing a home for my workshop for blocked artists and writers, and my students for their energy and enthusiasm. My deepest gratitude, however, goes to

Gunther Stuhlmann for support beyond the call of duty.

A final note: Those authors living and dead whose testimony is quoted here should be regarded neither as freaks nor as objects of sympathy for confessing openly to what so many others suffer from in relative secrecy. From the courage of their self-exposure, the rest of us draw consolation and hope for the future.

—Victoria Nelson
August 17, 1984

CHAPTER 1

WHAT IS WRITER'S BLOCK?

Without resistance you can do nothing.
—Jean Cocteau

If you are a writer who is not writing, you tend to think of yourself in a number of ways, all bad. You are, so you think, lazy, undisciplined, a shirker, a failure, a cowardly fraud, a good-for-nothing, et cetera, et cetera.

The phenomenon known as "writer's block"—the temporary or chronic inability to put words to paper—is almost universally regarded as a highly undesirable, not to mention unpleasant, experience. It has been called the "unnatural thwarting of what struggles to come into being, but cannot" (Tillie Olsen); the "pitiable instance of long incubation producing no chick" (George Eliot). Authors beyond count have bewailed the tortures of this condition, which seems to strike hardened veterans as frequently as it does beginners.

Being unable to write, however, or, for that matter, to perform any creative endeavor, is not bad in itself. Properly interpreted, writer's block is the best thing that can happen to a writer. Resistance to writing is a vital regulator of the creative process because it obliges us to suspend our plans and reconsider the nature of our relation to the creative forces inside us, forces that are, in the final analysis, gifts—ours by virtue of grace and not possession.

First, let's eliminate a common misconception. Writer's block is not a passive condition. It is an aggressive reaction, a loud shout from your unconscious calling your attention to the fact that something is out of adjustment. *The block is a signal to readjust the way you are approaching your work; it is not the problem itself.* Accepting and responding to the message of the block is the way in which every writer matures and receives the blessing of his unconscious self, the ultimate source of creativity.

As the poet Carolyn Kizer has said, "The unconscious creates, the ego edits." This is a simple way of describing the complex relationship between our thoughts and images in the unconscious—that side of our psyche not directly accessible to us—and the shaping that our conscious self, or ego (I will use these terms interchangeably), gives them once they emerge. Although resistance to the creative experience can take as many forms and spring from as many individual motives as there are writers and artists, the central meaning of writer's block remains constant: *Inability to write means your unconscious self is vetoing the program of your conscious ego.* Even as you seem to identify yourself totally with the side of you that says yes, another side of you is saying no even more forcefully.

Why "no"? Why the stubborn lack of cooperation? In desperation our egos manufacture dozens of reasons, mostly self-denigratory, to explain why creativity refuses to flow. But these stereotypical accusations, such as "procrastinator," are far from the truth. The key to the dilemma lies not in any failure of willpower—blocked writers, as we will see, usually have too much will—but in the relationship you have cultivated with your unconscious.

A writer who finds herself unable to produce has made no conscious choice not to write. The resistance is often experienced as a barrier that has arisen involuntarily, a literal block between the conscious self and its sources of material in the unconscious. The fact that the block seems involuntary means the source of resistance is not conscious; it lies, as it were, on the other side of the barrier—in the realm of the unconscious. This autonomous kingdom runs on its own rules, sometimes incomprehensible to the conscious ego. Break one of those rules, and it will cut off communication. The unconscious is a tough country with strong defenses; trying to muscle your way across the border won't work. Instead, you must work to reestablish diplomatic relations with your unconscious, a process of painstaking negotiation that may take a long, long time.

How does a writer get—and stay—on good terms with his creative partner, the unconscious? Before presenting some suggestions, I would like to make a short digression on the nature of creativity.

SELF-LOVE AND CREATIVITY

My own heart let me more have pity on; let
Me live to my sad self hereafter kind,
Charitable; not live this tormented mind
With this tormented mind tormenting yet.

—Gerard Manley Hopkins

What is creativity? Above all, it is *play*, the child's fresh spontaneity waiting to come forth in writing, or painting, or composing music, or any creative act.

Most creative persons—as well as most people generally—remember their childhoods as a time when they threw themselves wholeheartedly into all manner of creative efforts—drawing, storytelling, modeling in clay, whatever came to hand. Most important, they experienced no resistance to their play.

The adult writer who wants to recapture this joyful spirit from which all creativity springs must have the humility to recognize, first of all, that he has forgotten how to play. Luckily, learning how again is not that hard. You must simply start thinking like a child. If I want to play, for example, do I wait till semester break or summer vacation? Do I wait till I move to the country, away from noisy traffic? Do I wait till my children are grown? Hardly. The child in myself demands emphatically, "I want to have fun *now*. I don't want to wait, and I don't see why I should." Viewed from this perspective, procrastination simply means delaying pleasure, the pleasure to be gained from the playful act of creation.

Moreover, no one wants to have fun just occasionally. When I want to play, I want to play at least an hour every day, if not four or five. If I don't have at least one hour, I don't feel alive. I need it every day. I'm not putting my soul and joy on hold until some vague paradise materializes in my future. If I wait five years to have fun—whether to climb a tree or run down a beach or write—my muscles will be stiff and resistant. I will have throttled my spontaneous desire to play by not giving it free rein on an immediate, regular basis.

An important principle is evident here. Creative discipline grows out of pleasure, not out of tyranny or self-abuse. Those people who have a strong natural tendency to do what they *like* are those most likely to find discipline an easy responsibility to assume. Their overriding need to satisfy themselves is the solid foundation that sustains them during the long tedious years of training.

Even pleasure, though, can be perversely hard to reach. Many people find it difficult to head straight for their fun; something in them refuses to play. The barrier is not lack of willpower (did you ever need willpower, as a child, to make mud pies?), but a stronger and much more seductive emotion: hatred. Specifically, hatred of self.

Loving oneself—as opposed to the narcissism of being in love with oneself, with all its attendant insecurities—is one of the most difficult life tasks to master, and it is integrally related to the creative process.

Having survived the traumas of childhood and adolescence, during which self-loathing often reaches an irrational zenith, most of us find something or other worthy of appreciation in ourselves. But if it is merely an admission of meager merit, it is not self-love. Often, all we have learned as adults is how to hide, out of sheer self-protection, the extent of our own dis-ease; in the name of modesty and self-sacrifice, we go right on abusing ourselves.

Self-love, like writing itself, is not a static condition, but an *act* requiring positive moral energy. It is one of the obligations and potential joys of being human. The absence of love is not a neutral state. Nature abhors a vacuum, and love's opposite will move in to fill the empty space. Despair results from surrendering to the hateful inner voice that incessantly whispers, "You're no good." This self-hatred is a force that must be firmly countered, never given in to. To be free to play, you must have the strength to keep your demon at bay.

Why must one love oneself to write? Writing, like the other arts, is a fluid, dynamic process; there is nothing rote or mechanical about the act of creation. Carl Jung quotes a precept of medieval alchemy: *Ars requiret totum hominem,* "Art requires the presence of the total being." To keep the total being available means staying in constant touch with yourself. If you tap a large hidden reservoir of self-hatred every time you establish contact with your unconscious, you are not likely to want to stay in touch with yourself. In fact, the block springs up to shield you from this withering blast from within. The despised block is actually protecting you— in a primitive way, certainly, but in response to an even more primitive emotion. How else can you be protected if you refuse to acknowledge the deeper unease?

Learning to confront the demon directly instead of using the indirect defense of the block means, simply, that you must learn to love yourself. To function as a writer implies that you must, above all, love and honor your creative force, which might be pictured as a childlike spirit. You must be very gentle with this "creative child"; the younger it is, the gentler you must be. You must not chain your child in a dark closet or force it to perform distasteful chores. You must let it out to play, as all children desire to do; you must let it follow, with your loving guidance, its own inclination.

If you are harsh with your creative self and unreasonably demanding, you will eventually be stuck with a sullen, rebellious, never-to-mature adolescent who refuses to clean up his room or do the dishes; thus have you bred and reared your own creative soul. But if you have been a wise and gentle parent, your child will prosper and reward you in ways your narrow adult ego could never believe possible.

When you experience writer's block, it means your creative child is throwing herself on the floor and refusing to cooperate. What do you do under these circumstances? Do you try to compel your child, kicking and screaming, to do what she would not? Do you send her to her room without dinner? Do you give her a number of logical reasons why she *ought* to cooperate? Or do you try to find out why she doesn't want to in the first place?

The key is *what* you have asked your child to do and *how* you have asked. Have you only asked him to play? Are you sure you have not commanded him to perform brain surgery or recite Shakespeare? Have you enrolled him in Harvard when he, at the age of three, does not want to go? In other words, have you imposed unrealistic expectations on a creature whose true potential may lie in a direction totally overlooked by you? Who, in fact, is the real child here?

This classic conflict between the ego and the unconscious demonstrates an interesting fact: We tend to be much kinder to other people—our friends, relatives, and offspring—than we are to ourselves, to whom, in the dingy privacy of our own inner lives, we often behave like little dictators and dictatresses. Nine times out of ten, writer's block is the child's healthy scream of pain or rebellion against outrageous totalitarian treatment or blasting self-hatred, which are only two sides of the same sad coin. When you are internally polarized in this way, it is impossible for your ego to perform the fine discrimination and weighing of unconscious messages that are vital to the creative effort.

Discipline must be acquired eventually, but it is not to be perverted to another occasion for self-loathing. True creative discipline—and productivity—blossoms in conditions of gentleness and respect. It should be further noted that the conditions of creativity are not synonymous with its results: Self-love is not the same as adopting a tone of optimism in your work. Gloomy, despairing works of art as well as "cheerful" ones are the product of a positive relationship between conscious and unconscious in the artist's psyche. And those writers, like Kafka, whose self-esteem was not measurably high, who have still managed, despite great suffering and self-torture, to produce a body of significant work, can be said to have triumphed over their own disabilities. They have experienced self-integration in the creative act itself.

To maintain the delicate equilibrium between ego and unconscious, each writer needs to give careful attention to the unique nature of her own creative self. Sometimes you must tear up the application to Harvard (i.e., an overambitious project) as being beyond your child's capabilities. Other times, you must realize that, out of a critical lack of self-confidence, you have forced your Harvard-educated creative energies to endure the ignominy of kindergarten!

In short, it is necessary to employ your conscious ego to distinguish between the infantile destructive child*ish* and the inspired, playful, child*like* workings of your unconscious. Only by a meticulous "sorting of the seeds," as the Jungians say—into wheat or chaff—can we determine the appropriate creative response to each situation.

Such careful discrimination is not possible if we do not love ourselves. In cases of self-hatred, the ego is likely to turn from a sensitive guide into an interfering tyrant. Paradoxically, only affection yields the balance and detachment needed to understand and judge the messages we receive from the unconscious.

Think of tapping your creative gifts as you would establishing a relation with another person. If you try to possess or control that person, he or she will elude you; if you form a friendship based on mutual respect, over time, with much love and patience, you can forge a secure bond. To accomplish this goal, however, you must be prepared to effect a fundamental change of attitude toward yourself. At the root of all practical prescriptions must be a spiritual turning around, an opening up to new possibilities in the self, an infusion of that positive spirit without which all life activities seem as they did to Hamlet, "stale, flat, unprofitable."

Such a metamorphosis will not take place as a result of a New Year's resolution. Love, of oneself as much as of another, remains an act of grace, not a conscious, willed decision. It is something to be relaxed into, not compelled. When the miracle happens (and it is an easy miracle, if you will only allow it) you will find a different reality before you. With your eyes newly opened you will see that what seemed at first a barrier—your resistance—is actually the secret door to your unconscious. Hurl yourself against it and you will only succeed in bruising yourself. Approach with love and careful attention, and it will open of its own accord. This is the way you discover that your writer's block is actually a building block in your unfolding development as an artist.

CHAPTER 2

STARTING COLD:
Beginner's Block

> *Times of growth are beset with difficulties. They re-*
> *semble a first birth. But these difficulties arise from the*
> *very profusion of all that is struggling to attain form.*
> *Everything is in motion; therefore, if one perseveres*
> *there is a prospect of great success, in spite of the exist-*
> *ing danger.*
> —Richard Wilhelm, Commentary on the *I Ching*,
> Hexagram 3, "Difficulty at the Beginning"

Let's begin at the beginning. The problem facing most writers who are just setting out and many experienced writers as well is simply this: Why is it so hard to start writing? And why, especially, is it so hard to *start* to start?

As I sit at my typewriter facing an empty page, a thousand thoughts race through my head. Out of that whirling grab bag of possibilities, how do I make a decision? How do I *choose*, pick one word or the other, violate the virgin blankness of the paper with a pitifully inadequate rendering of my complex imaginings? No. I decide that it is easier to keep the thoughts in my mind, spare the snowy white paper, avoid the discouraging compromise between intent and technical ability that is the written word.

So goes a certain mood familiar to all who would and do write. This gentle daydream, however, is itself the true violation of a writer's spirit and talent. The bravest act a writer can perform is to take that tiny step forward, put down the wretched little word that pricks the balloon of inflated fantasies with its very mundanity, and then put down another word directly after it. This act marks the decision to be a *writer.* That first word put on paper bridges the gulf between the person who imagines what it is like to write and the person who writes.

Not everyone with a desire to write, after all, becomes a writer. That is not necessarily because of lack of inherent talent or ability to communicate with words. Many avid readers, for example, harbor a secret desire to be a writer because they believe that the pleasure to be gained from writing is identical to that gained from reading. But to be a writer, a person must first actually write, and write a great deal.

Does this definition sound simpleminded? Then consider: A long-distance runner is someone who runs. Runs long distances, in fact. A long-distance runner is not a person who *desires* to run. And not only does a long-distance runner actually run, he or she probably does so every day. If I announce to my friends that I want to run the Boston Marathon, they might reasonably ask, "What steps are you taking to achieve this goal?" I might answer, "Well, I'm training ten miles every other day this year. I want to run a few fourteen-kilometer races first to see how I do under pressure. Next year I'll increase my training to fifteen miles. If I can maintain that distance at a good time for another year, maybe then I'll be ready."

But suppose I answer instead, "I'm not running at all right now. I just thought I'd like to try it." Pressed further, I admit, "I thought I'd start with the Boston Marathon to see if I like running or not."

My friends might justifiably consider me not merely mad but a likely candidate for shin splints or a heart attack. Just think, then, how benevolently we let slide in casual conversation that famous wish-announcement: "I've got a novel in me. Someday I'm going to write it."

I'm not attacking here the earnest desire to communicate to others a life story full of hard-won truths. I do argue, however, with the image. A novel is something that stands at the end of a lengthy process called writing. It is not a pre-existing Platonic form embedded within you, only waiting to emerge on the page (or, as some would have it, to be "dialogued"). I do not have a Boston Marathon inside me waiting to get out. The Boston Marathon is a peak experience I am rightly entitled to look forward to only as the culmination of regular training and love of running.

But running, you say, is essentially a matter of performance; it is not a creative act. If writing were really only a matter of putting one foot in front of the other, there would be no

writer's block. This is true. Creation, however, *is* performance. It can be argued that you are not so much "translating"
an idea in your head into words as you are creating the idea in
the shape of the words that present themselves to you. As the
poet William Stafford has said, "A writer is not so much
someone who has something to say as he is someone who has
found a process that will bring about new things he would not
have thought of if he had not started to say them."

The words, in effect, create the idea. The result—play,
story, poem—is the record of your act of creation. It is emphatically not a prize you can capture once you get through
the tedium of "dialoguing." The chores *are* the prize.
They're it. They're all you get.

The novel as modern Americans think of it is composed
of roughly ten thousand carefully crafted sentences. The
shaping of each and every one of those sentences is what the
craft of writing is all about. As Philip Roth has his distinguished author declare in *The Ghost Writer:*

> "I turn sentences around. That's my life. I write a sentence and
> then I turn it around. Then I look at it and I turn it around
> again. Then I have lunch. Then I come back in and write an-
> other sentence. Then I have tea and turn the new sentence
> around. Then I read the two sentences over and turn them
> both around. Then I lie down on my sofa and think. Then I
> get up and throw them out and start from the beginning. And
> if I knock off from this routine for as long as a day, I'm frantic
> with boredom and a sense of waste. . . ."

This is the nuts and bolts of the writing experience. And you
must love (or perhaps more accurately, be compelled into)
repeating this narrow and exacting task ten thousand times
before you will have produced a novel.

Once again I have mentioned the word *love*. This type
of love, however, is directed toward an activity as well as to-

ward oneself. How can I run a marathon if I don't intrinsically love the act of running for its own sake? Only the fact that I love to run—to the end of the block, down the beach, whenever I can seize the opportunity—will carry me through the years of grinding practice necessary to develop my running powers to their full capacity. The core of the running or writing experience is pleasure in the act. It sweetens the tedium of training, it carries me on lighthearted to my goal.

Still, let's face it. It's a terrible, anxiety-ridden moment, that first encounter with the blank page, whether you are facing it for the first time or after an extended absence from the discipline of writing. Of all the types of writer's block, "starting cold" is arguably the most formidable. If, as is likely, your eye is fixed on the end of the marathon and you are not firmly centered in the joy and rigor of that first step or sentence *in itself,* you are likely to stumble and fall.

Starting cold is usually a *developmental* block; with time and training, it often falls away. (Later chapters will cover *chronic,* or recurring, blocks and *situational* blocks that grow out of a specific writing context.)

For many, this first experience of writer's block is definitive. They get right up from the desk and never come back, and they are correct and honest to do so. Their inner child has sent them a message so unmistakable that they would be foolish and wrongheaded to persevere or to experience a moment's guilt for their decision. For this large and honorable portion of the population, the writer's block, properly interpreted, opens a door to a bright future, albeit a different one than they had anticipated: It has told them that, despite the demands of their ego, there is *something else* out there they would rather be doing than writing. And they are now free to go find this thing, and do it.

Others are slower on the uptake. Camped at the doorstep of writing, blocked from entry but unable to make the decision to turn away, they become the true Ancient Mariners of the writing world. Persons stalemated permanently in such a position (that is, before they have written enough to qualify as *writers* with writer's block) tend to display this symptom as the tip of the iceberg, so to speak, of a more generalized compulsive neurosis in which—to make a long story relatively short—the desire to perform a given act is pitted against the inability to do so. Such an impasse is often linked to a fear of maturity and accomplishment. The ultimate goal of this elaborately designed ritual is to increase the self-loathing of the sufferer and divert his or her attention from the true source of misery, which is generally something entirely removed from the writing sphere.

For example, there is the case of a man who, coming late to college, was driven by compulsive fears that he had failed in life and always would. Accordingly, he set out to master every scrap of learning material that came his way. He quickly fell under the spell of two books he was assigned in literature classes, those talismans of the sixties, *Lord of the Flies* and *Steppenwolf*. Immersing himself in these works, he devised an elaborate theory that explained both the books and his own relation to the universe. At term's end, however, he found himself completely unable to convey this complex tangle of interlocking ideas in the medium of two five-page reports. He was unable, in fact, to set down a single sentence from his well-thumbed stack of index cards. (For a fuller treatment of the note-taking phenomenon, see Chapter 8.) Taking incompletes in both courses, he tortured himself nightly for several years poring fruitlessly over the books and his notes, hopelessly blocked. The papers were never written. What he had cleverly hit upon, in fact, was a way to carry over his deep self-loathing into the academic environment, where he had actually begun to show signs of promise in areas other than writing. His true source of misery was not writing but a more extensive personality confusion that chose this specific outlet as a way of dramatizing to him that his whole life was "blocked."

As different from the average writer's experience as it may be, this extreme syndrome has unpleasant echoes we all recognize, for two reasons: (1) Almost every writer, at the outset of his or her creative adventure, has at least briefly fallen victim to this type of obsessive behavior, and (2) it is a chilling illustration of the paralysis that may result at any stage of a writer's career when a writer's block is not positively resolved.

For most of us, however, it's the shock of using new muscles, of having no idea what they're capable of, that freezes us at the outset. The less you have done of something, after all, the harder it is to do. This initial painful hesitation is a function of development; it is something we outgrow as we become more facile with the written word. The block and the stage fright that produces it are literally written away as you slowly develop your skills. For this easing to take place, however, you must step over the threshold: You must begin to write. There is no other way.

COMING BACK TO WRITING

What of the person who has done a great deal of writing in the past but has put it aside a number of years? Or the person who comes new to writing late in life? In *Silences,* the fiction writer Tillie Olsen has written vividly of the block that comes from long delay or postponement of the writing adventure:

> The habits of a lifetime when everything else had to come before writing are not easily broken, even when circumstances now often make it possible for writing to be first; habits of years—response to others, distractibility, responsibility for daily matters—stay with you, mark you, become you. The cost of "discontinuity" (that pattern still imposed on women) is such a weight of things unsaid, an accumulation of material

so great, that everything starts up something else in me; what should take weeks, takes me sometimes months to write; what should take months, takes years.

This is a gloomy predicament, but not devoid of hope. First of all, comfort yourself with the knowledge that although a marathon runner might be able to run your two-mile course in eight minutes, it is going to take you considerably longer, because you are out of shape. A person who is out of shape is in the same boat as a person who has never been in shape at all. You cannot impose expectations from your past, when you were in shape, onto the present, when you are not.

It takes a certain amount of humility to realize this, but humility is a far more freeing attitude than the brand of self-criticism that attacks you for failing to maintain standards from a previous era in your life. If you have left off piano playing for twenty years, you do not sit down and attempt Liszt or Mendelssohn. You start with scales, slowly, until your hands begin to remember the way. You must realize that, starting late, you may never reach or regain the technical proficiency required to play Liszt, but what you can play within your natural limits you play very well.

The key once again is to focus on the first word or sentence you are putting down. Do not look back, to what might have been, or forward, to what may never happen. Concentrate on the moment of composition. After you have written your first sentence, go on to the next. Nothing else in the world except you and that sentence exists. Remember that your muscles are stiff and must be slowly relaxed, not forced, into the task. While it may be true that you no longer possess the energy of earlier years or that life has indeed hardened you into attitudes that dam up an easy flow of words, still you possess the supreme advantage that is usually lacking in youth: patience. And patience is the most valuable quality a writer can have.

VOICES FROM THE PAST

Suppose, though, that the threshold proves to be a formidable barrier, not a gateway. What inhibits that first necessary step? One common difficulty might be called "voices from the past."

True writer's block is not a phenomenon of childhood. A child either writes spontaneously because she likes to—stories, reports, poetry—or doesn't write because she doesn't like to; as a rule, young children don't complain of, say, wanting to fingerpaint but finding themselves mysteriously unable to do so.

In school, however, things can take a bad turn, and frequently an overcritical or narrow teacher can freeze a child's natural instincts toward self-expression. Many highly literate people can trace their dislike of writing to a critical teacher or unresponsive parent.

Such people, when they are not writers by profession, have neither the incentive nor the necessity, for that matter, to overcome a block that rests at the periphery of their lives. They may have difficulty writing memos, letters, or whatever, but the block in these cases is simply a minor annoyance. On the other hand, *writers* who have internalized a witch or tyrant from their pasts who despises their every word have the obligation to face up to this childhood ghost. For although it is right and totally justified that a child should feel terrified of such a real person in his life, a grown-up does not need to feel the same way thirty years later. Those of us who continue to clutch on to a Nasty Teacher or Critical Parent after we have become, theoretically, self-regulating individuals are granting self-loathing a very convenient and pernicious entrée into our inner lives. Who, after all, can help having an awful father or mother? Poor me!

But when I am sitting in my room "trying" to write, as we like to say, who is actually physically present? Not Mr. X or Mrs. Y, certainly, if they are even alive at all. The only one in that room is—me. And the only honest conclusion I can draw from this undeniable fact is that *I*, a part of me, is Mr. X or Mrs. Y, and that part of me hates me and is my mortal enemy. Period.

I must take responsibility for generating this hatred and criticism myself before I can ever hope to get past it. As long as it is attached to some cardboard figure from the past, my demon has succeeded in fooling me and I will never be able to confront him/her directly. (More on this subject in Chapter 4.)

GETTING SERIOUS

So much for childhood ghosts. Assuming that these are, if not actually exorcised, at least not actively bothering you, what are the more ordinary fears and mental quirks that are likely to restrain you from plunging right in with your writing? A common one is the fallacy of "getting serious." Persons who have reached a point in their lives in which they wish to focus their interest seriously on writing and concentrate on developing their abilities often paradoxically experience this moment as expulsion from Eden. The apple has been bitten; self-consciousness enters the picture. You decide, to your eternal loss, that henceforth you are no longer to Play, you are to Write.

This decision has a silencing effect on your creative child, who still wants nothing more than to keep on playing. He does not want to be sent to military school, and he refuses to cooperate in this mad plan. That is the message he sends back to you, in the form of a writer's block, when you suddenly interrupt his play by rapping out a command to Write.

What is the best response to this situation? Here, I think, the answer is unequivocal: You apologize deeply to your child, throw away the little uniform, and give him back his toys. You do not try to make your fragile budding talent carry prematurely the extra weight of Seriousness. (This advice applies equally to experienced writers, who can paralyze themselves with an exaggerated sense of their own importance.)

Translated into the reality of your writing life, what does giving back the toys mean? It means that, for example, you will not try to switch your accustomed mode of expression for another that seems more "lofty" and befitting a great writer. You will not forswear the style you have already developed because somebody else (or more likely you yourself) thinks it doesn't sound the way it "should." You have already traveled down the path a long way, in fact, just to be able to write in the way you do. Your new sense of commitment must not be allowed to change the nature of what you are doing, nor hasten its growth artificially. Your writing will develop much more naturally if you resist the temptation, for the time being, to crown yourself Writer and continue to think of yourself as someone who is just playing around. Remember that the despised word "dilettante" comes from *diletto,* delight or joy!

THE QUESTION OF TIME

Another important early step in becoming a writer is learning how to allocate *time* in your life for writing. Time is a critical factor in the evolution of a writer. Abuse of time, moreover, is more likely to inhibit writing than any other single factor.

Most writers believe that abuse of time means not spending enough time working. I believe the reverse. I believe we abuse time far more often by attempting to be unrealistically strict with ourselves than by being too lax. Laziness or procrastination in writing is almost always the direct response to an internal edict that is far too severe. It is the same yo-yo behavior apparent in the dieting/overeating phenomenon. Instead of embarking on a positive program of healthy eating, dedicated dieters put themselves on a *gulag* routine of fasting with occasional breaks for carrots and broth. This extreme maltreatment of the organism produces, in time, its antithesis: an orgy of chocolate-cake eating. Similarly, the attempt to impose on oneself a stringent regime of writing usually produces its direct opposite, no writing at all. The psyche revolts against harsh new habits.

This block may also strike those who write at sporadic times of day—who, given the choice of any time at all to write, will closet themselves with coffee and cigarettes, say, from Friday morning to Tuesday afternoon, instead of going out and having fun on the weekend like any right-minded individual. Often the body and emotions rebel against this forced labor by refusing to let their master or mistress write again for a long, unpredictable period of time. And then, the whole cycle may start up again. There is much to be said, in terms of plain animal comfort, for being a nine-to-fiver in the literary world.

Beginners are often the most unrealistic in their use of time, if only because their expectations of what they will be able to produce are as yet untested. They have still to learn their natural capacity and rhythm in writing. If you have Gotten Serious to boot, you are likely to abandon your unselfconscious writing patterns of the past and embark on an overambitious program that can freeze you up harder than Lake Baikal.

Many beginning writers work sporadically at first. This is the natural way to ease yourself into a creative medium. Gradually you will gather momentum. Over time, this rhythm settles into a semiregular routine, but it is often not until five to seven years of serious writing have passed that you are equal to (and more important, *look forward to*) a daily routine. During those years your child has had the time and space, thanks to your gentle care, to mature into a staunch ally, not a lazy, rebellious indentured servant.

It is for this reason that—to part company with the old adage—inspiration and not perspiration may have to be your guide at the beginning. You must write when you *want* to write, keeping as close to your original pursuit of pleasure and the spirit of play as possible. As your writing muscles develop at their own not-to-be-hurried rate—perhaps quickly but far more likely slowly—you will find yourself able to write with greater technical facility. This increase in your powers produces a tremendous feeling of pleasure and accomplishment, which in turn motivates you in the best possible way (and far more solidly than outside praise) to persevere in your efforts.

The single most common mistake in setting up a writing schedule—one that, unbelievably, even experienced writers con themselves into committing—is to say to yourself: "Well, my schedule is too full at the moment to do any writing, unfortunately. But come semester break/summer vacation/retirement/Christmas, I will have eight hours a day to write, write, write!"

Surely no faster way to trigger a writing block has yet been devised by humankind. Comes the long-awaited time, the eager neophyte sits down at the typewriter and—nothing. A total blank.

Why? Because, after cutting out all training (and fun) for a lengthy period of time, you are sitting down to the emotional and creative equivalent of the Boston Marathon. Inside you the child is writhing in anguish that you have so mistreated her by setting such a difficult task. Run the marathon cold? No, thanks!

How, then, is a busy schedule to be unraveled to allow time for writing? Here, as in Chapter 1, I should point out that if you genuinely like to write, you will find time for it as a matter of course. As Fritz Perls, the cofounder of Gestalt therapy, has said: "The organism does not *make decisions*.

The organism works always on the basis of *preference*."
Nevertheless, logic and planning can be used in pursuing
preference. Visualize the following questions and alternative
responses as a kind of decision making flowchart:

> Question 1. Can unnecessary items be cut out of my
> busy schedule to give me time to write?

If your answer is yes, you have your time. If it is no, proceed
to the next question:

> Question 2. Is my schedule going to be this full for the
> next year?

If your answer is no, then wait until the time opens up. Less
than a year is an acceptable waiting time (but just barely). If
your answer is yes, proceed to:

> Question 3. Have I in fact made an existential choice,
> i.e., decided *against* writing as part of my
> daily experience, just by having this kind
> of life?

If your answer is yes, ask yourself:

> Question 4. What unrealized hopes/fantasies does my
> desire to write actually stand for, and how
> can they be realized in my life *as I am liv-
> ing it this very moment?*

It's important to realize that "wanting to write" is a time-
honored fantasy for many, equivalent to escaping to a desert
island. This is harmless daydreaming that only turns ugly
when you begin judging your fantasy by real-world standards that patently don't apply: I keep thinking about writing

but never do it, therefore I'm a failure and a fraud. Then it is time to ask yourself what gap in your real life this fantasy is a substitute for. Often it is simply freedom from daily responsibilities and a sterile work environment. These constraints can be eased in ways entirely unrelated to writing, which carries its own staggering set of daily responsibilities and drudgery.

But let's move back to Question 3. What if you answered no? What if you are determined to write in spite of an overwhelmingly busy life? Some—very few—take responsibility for their time allocations in the following way: "I must keep this schedule because other lives depend on my earning a livelihood, but in spite of all odds I will carve out an hour or two every day for myself because I *want* to write." This decision requires sacrifice, stamina, and a special kind of courage to keep the playful creative child alive and happy. It represents a critical turning point at which a small number of developing writers emerge from the ranks of those who merely desire to write.

A ROOM OF ONE'S OWN

Virginia Woolf listed as a primary requirement of the writer an inviolable space in which to be alone with one's thoughts and words. There is no question that for many writers this space is utterly essential to their development. Very few writers have been able to go about their business successfully with other people in the same room performing their daily tasks. (Jane Austen is one of the exceptions that prove the rule.) But you do not need to be too narrowly literal or literary in interpreting what this space should be in your life.

A desk where your writing and typewriter are permanently set out certainly can be a soothing talismanic object that protects you against the fear that comes at the beginning. All the preliminaries of getting paper and notes discourage some writers; taking off the typewriter cover can sometimes feel like opening King Tut's sarcophagus. It's easier to start playing if the toys are already laid out.

Some writers, feeling a need for greater privacy, rent rooms or garages in other homes, go to writer's colonies, or wind up in the proverbial cabin in the woods. While these alternatives work—are in fact an absolute necessity—for some, they definitely do not work for all. Even for an experienced writer, it can be as risky to divorce the place of your writing from your regular life as it is to divorce the time. This restriction of your writing to a region vacuum-sealed from your daily affairs tends to give it that dreaded "special" aura that can lead to a first-class writer's block. The formidable weight of literary tradition hits you as soon as you walk into the pristine sanctum lacking telephone, dirty socks, newspapers, all the comforting links to the outside world. Most writers need strong, enduring emotional and social ties in daily life to balance the inner solitude. (Walden Pond, after all, was in easy walking distance of Concord.) Writing is a lonely vocation. By putting yourself into a lonely environment as well, you risk turning Prospero's cell into a padded one.

Often the illusion persists that if one weren't surrounded by family, duty, business, and other distractions, a great flood of creativity would be released. Getting away from the routines and setting of the ordinary can often have a wonderfully vivifying effect on your work—and your spirits. But when you finally get to the writer's colony, you may be crushed to discover that your surroundings make no difference at all—that you continue to put in the same hour a day or less that you did with all the chaos of daily life around you. If you are this kind of writer, you have made an important discovery: You are not *blocked* simply because you write only so much per day. This is your internal rhythm or setpoint that functions regardless of your environment. Learn to value and accept it.

If you are still determined to try your cabin in the woods, consider taking a spouse or friend with you. It is often a mistake to go entirely by yourself. As any peasant can tell you, the wilderness is full of demons that feed on the souls of solitary humans. If you are going only to chop wood and set up a primitive living situation, you are not likely to be bothered by them, being too occupied with material concerns. But if you are going with the sole intent of tuning into your unconscious, you may be swallowed up by what comes out. Moreover, you may be bored and frustrated—what else is there for you to do, after all? Writing is not a twenty-four-hour occupation.

Though many writers do flourish in this setting, it's important to realize that the cabin in the woods stereotype is just that—a collective shoe that may not fit your foot. If it pinches, why force yourself to wear it? Often such attempts at isolating yourself are merely another disguise for your ego's efforts to *compel,* rather than allow, writing. You think: Up there with nothing else to do, I'll have to write, right? Wrong. Far from being alone with your work, you are much more likely to be alone with your compulsion *not* to write.

Many joys are to be derived from the early stages of writing. For one, you are not yet broken into the yoke of a writing career, and thus you can enjoy all its spiritual rewards with none of its real-world responsibilities. You have not yet begun to worry about repeating yourself. You are experimenting. You are truly writing for yourself, and no one else.

During these early years, as you are discovering how, what, and under which conditions you prefer to write, keep your attention firmly fixed on the excitement and difficulties of each moment of writing, of the specific problem you are grappling with or the passage you were able to bring up to its fullest level of expression—and what a triumph that is. After all, you are in the process of limbering up and toning your creative muscles. Relax and enjoy it. Do not try to look too far ahead, or you will be paralyzed by the prospect of possible achievements you are not nearly ready to make. Respect your own efforts, feeble as they will undoubtedly strike you from time to time. Most writers start from zero, and it is far easier to get better than to get worse.

Above all, remember that attitude is far more important than time or place. Do your writing where and when you *prefer*. Approach writing as a duty, a hallowed mission, or a vehicle for your need to be important, and your desire to write will shrivel inside you. Approach writing in a relaxed manner, and your desire will not desert you.

WARMING UP: CHILD'S PLAY*

There is an easy remedy for the difficulty of "starting cold": warming up!

Warming up consists of the following steps:

FIRST, allow yourself to do nothing at all until you feel a deep and genuine urge to write something.

THEN:

1. Write only *what* you want to.
2. Write *where* and *when* you want to.
3. Write as much or as little as you like.
4. When you get tired of writing, quit.

Perform this exercise faithfully whenever you experience resistance writing according to a preconceived blueprint and/or regimen.

Warm up with any kind of writing that comes easily. Record your dreams if they interest you. Write about your last (or first) love affair. Start a journal. What's important to remember is that you're just fooling around. What you're doing isn't serious. It's not part of a professional trip. It "doesn't count." It's play.

Make believe you are a child again, doing *only* what you love to do, what gives you pleasure. Go always in the direction in which you instinctively feel the strongest pull, regardless of whether or not your ego judges this to be the "right" sort of writing. Your instincts and your talent want to flow in this direction, so let them—let the river find its natural course. Whatever you create, make sure the experience gives you the most possible satisfaction and fun. Indulge yourself completely.

---

*This is your first exercise. If you are chronically blocked, even the word "exercise" may be enough to cause resistance, or at least a flurry of inner panic. Never fear. *All* the exercises in this book are optional. Do only those that attract you.

PRO-CRASTINATION: Laziness Is *Not* the Issue

In the meantime I had got myself entangled in the old sorities of the old sophist—procrastination. I had suffered my necessary business to accumulate so terribly that I neglected to write to any one, till the pain I suffered from not writing made me waste as many hours in dreaming about it as would have sufficed for the letter-writing of half a life.

—Samuel Taylor Coleridge

Suppose you are past the "starting block." Suppose you have begun to write seriously and have accumulated a small but growing body of work. You are still troubled, however, by a nagging resistance to getting down to it. Worse yet, suppose—and this is by no means an uncommon experience—you have spent the last twenty-five or thirty years trying, in effect, to "push the river," because your personal river of creativity, contrary to all natural laws, shows no signs of wanting to flow by itself. What work you have actually managed to finish either stands as a sweaty monument to willpower or was produced, seemingly by accident, in various unscheduled moments of grace that no amount of wishing or forcing seems to be able to conjure up again.

Over the long haul, if resistance to writing develops into a chronic state, it becomes far more difficult to resolve than beginner's block. By this point, writer's block has hardened into an ingrained response, as habitual as smoking or overeating, and it must be approached at a correspondingly deep level in the psyche—a level that such devices as the New Year's resolution never penetrate. In fact, as we will see, the New Year's resolution, a.k.a. "willpower," plays an integral part in perpetuating the whole frustrating cycle. Writer's block is far more commonly found in the presence of too much, not too little, will.

There is a terrible perversity—one the blocked writer is all too aware of—about not doing what you must want to do. Yet once again, *not* wanting to write is, under certain crucial circumstances, as healthy and natural an impulse as the act of writing itself.

Notice that I have said "not wanting" to write. Usually the sufferer phrases it differently: "I want to write, but I *can't.*" For our purposes, it is more productive to accept the block for precisely what it is and say, "At the moment I don't *want* to write." Only by taking direct responsibility for this state of affairs can you proceed to (1) discover *why* you don't want to write—no, why you *refuse* to write (there is almost always an excellent reason that is a credit to your unconscious integrity)—and then (2) determine if an alternative path to writing is available. Although some of the reasons you will uncover seem on the surface to derive from specific technical problems you are experiencing with a manuscript, the deepest, most pervasive cause of chronic writer's block has nothing whatever to do with writing itself.

What is this cause? Let us first start with what it is not. It is most assuredly *not* procrastination. Here, I know, voices will rise in protest, "Are you crazy? Everybody knows that procrastination—simple downright laziness—is the root of writer's block." "Procrastination" is probably the catchall description of creative resistance most widely offered by writers. Procrastination is so eloquently evoked, so humorously described, so fervently cursed, that surely any effort to overcome writer's block must involve pinning this monster of slothful inactivity to the mat by its allegorical opposite, Willpower, right?

Wrong. To believe so only reinforces the trap you are caught in. First of all, attributing your resistance to laziness is judging yourself with unwarranted harshness. Most practicing writers who suffer from writer's block are extremely hardworking, not to say compulsive, souls. For such a person to tell himself he is a lazy good-for-nothing is patently untrue, but it is paradoxically easier to accept than to try to raise out of inner darkness the tangle of conflicting orders, counterorders, and outright mutiny raging in the bunker of his soul.

"Procrastinate," from the Latin *pro* ("forward") plus *crastinus* ("of tomorrow"), signifies literally "putting forward until tomorrow." Originally, the term was descriptive, not judgmental, a neutral word meaning simply "postponement." Although procrastination now frequently has a pejorative connotation, it does not describe a motive. To say you procrastinate in no way explains *why* you do so. "Laziness" and "lack of self-discipline" are glosses supplied by your ever-obliging demon. To say you don't write because you procrastinate is the same as saying you are sick because you don't feel well; it is a tautology, not a diagnosis.

Placing the word in its proper perspective—namely, as just another way of saying "writer's block"—lets us examine the true nature of procrastination. In common usage, it might best be described as a state of determined, though tortured, inactivity. Inactivity is usually viewed as a passive condition. In fact, however, it is as clear-cut an action as shooting skeet or flying to the moon; it represents the *decision* not to act. ("One must also decide to hesitate," as the Polish writer Stanislaw Jerzy Lec has aptly noted.) The highly active nature of procrastination becomes clear as we realize that it means *to push a task away from yourself*. Now, a task cannot be pushed away unless it has first been put forward in some form or another, and here we come to the real nature of procrastination: It is a *reaction*.

But a reaction to what? Take note of what has already been said about the nature of writer's block: that it is a *healthy reaction of the organism to an inner state of imbalance*. Procrastination is no limp failure of will; it is an exasperated protest.

The unconscious refusal to write is always based on sound principles; this truth cannot be repeated too often. When you announce to yourself and the world that you are a hopeless procrastinator, when you berate yourself for inertia or lack of moral fiber, you are casting aspersions on your own deepest impulses. This habit of self-hatred sets up a destructive division between your conscious personality and your (often) unconscious instincts, creating a permanent condition of war within your psyche which can never be resolved unless both sides agree to lay down arms.

—Unless both sides agree. Accomplishing this task is not nearly as easy as it sounds, because you will always be tempted to use the old neurotic way in hopes of achieving the new healthy results. "Right," you say, "I will *stop* this nonsense at once." But that is an ego command, and ego commands are not only doomed to failure in this situation, they are what got you into it in the first place. Resistance is almost never overcome forcibly; force almost always hardens and entrenches it.

Thus it is equally a myth that "willpower" is the sovereign cure for "procrastination." On the contrary, willpower, representing as it does an ego command, is often the true villain. Lifting the block is an *effort*less process; it does not involve your will.

Remember the old story about the contest between the wind and the sun? Each wagered they could make a man take off his overcoat first. The wind blew fiercely, but the man only held his coat shut harder. Then the sun shone, and the man gladly took off his coat. This is the difference between exerting willpower on your unconscious and letting it bask in your gentle acceptance.

The starting point for understanding why you procrastinate is to treat yourself with enough respect to assume that behind your inactivity lies an excellent, if not readily apparent, reason. And this reason is to be found in an altogether different attitude or trait *inside yourself* that precipitated your procrastinatory rejection.

Why do I say "inside yourself"? Why don't I mention backfiring cars, the booming stereo bass from the apartment next door, babies crying, phones ringing, malfunctioning typewriters, and all the myriad other external distractions that so concern blocked writers and counselors helping blocked writers find the "right environment"?

Because if these factors were really significant, you would have to float in a John Lilly sensory-deprivation tank to find total relief for your writer's block, an environment in which, if you tried to plug in your electric typewriter, you might find yourself permanently relieved of the problem. Ask yourself how many times, having created the "perfect environment," you have found yourself still hopelessly blocked. Even Proust had problems in his cork-lined bedchamber.

Beyond a reasonable point, therefore, external irritations represent nothing more than a projection of internal conflict onto the world. They are in no way *causes*. It is, in fact, the inner environment that needs some work and attention.

So we are back to the question: What is writer's block a reaction *to?* What is the unknown factor that provokes such a highly visible and aggravating response?

The nature of the invisible stimulus can be partly deduced from the extremely emotional and hostile nature of the reaction. For however much you may see it as a kind of passive paralysis, procrastination, or writer's block, is a very aggressive act: a pushing away, a rejection.

What in particular is likely to have triggered this repulsion within you? The nature of the writing you have set yourself to do? The severity of your deadline? The difficulty of turning your notes into prose? The unrealistic goals of perfection you aspire to? We will explore these specific issues later, but in most cases of chronic block, it is not what you want to write, or deadlines, or the like that is stopping you. It is the *nature of the command to write.* How have you presented your desire to write to your creative child—or, if you prefer, your unconscious self? Have you asked or have you commanded? Have you given him a choice of projects? Have you given him the choice of when, where, and how to write the project, or have you (having so little faith in yourself, your abilities, and your natural creative rhythm) screamed:

"Get busy this instant, or else!"

To this directive the creative child has one, and only one, response: "Forget it!"

Tragically, this stubborn rebellion by your unconscious usually triggers even more severe and desperate measures from you, its hapless guardian, to impose a strict regimen of work: total isolation, nine-hour days, endless changes of locale and paraphernalia. But it is all for nothing. Attempts to be ruthless with yourself in order to "overcome procrastination" must always lead directly back to the hated condition itself, engendering stalemate. Even a reasonable order, *if it is an order,* will be rejected. The sense of failure and frustration increases by another order of magnitude as the vicious circle clicks back into gear.

People who accuse themselves of procrastination are not procrastinators. They are accusers. Far from being lazy, they are driven by such extremes of self-distrust and compulsive overcontrol that they throttle the spontaneous contact with self that all creative activity requires. The analogy with overeating is again apt: Just as chronic overeaters are not typically fun-loving, greedy sensualists but starved creatures desperately and (let it be said) spitefully rebelling against the tyrant inside them who is ordering them to be thin, so procrastinators are not lazy good-for-nothings but rather, as a rule, excessively conscientious strivers, overwhelmed by their own self-demands.

What came first in this chicken-and-egg situation is unimportant. What matters, once this conflict has become an entrenched feature of your personality, is the dynamics of the control-rebellion impasse and how to get out of it. For if you see yourself as a procrastinator, you are suffering from an altogether different disease than laziness.

Let us now leave the bogus issue of procrastination and move to the real inner conflict it masks.

SELF-LABELING

If you habitually think of yourself as a procrastinator (as most blocked writers do), take a sheet of paper and try the following exercise:

On the left-hand side of the page, write down all the negative labels you apply to yourself during a period of creative resistance: (e.g. "neurotic fraud," "spineless," "lazy"—pick your favorite). On the right-hand side, write down all the positive labels you apply to yourself as a writer.

Now compare the columns. Note two points: (1) The person described on the left and the person described on the right inhabit the same body. (2) You may have far fewer descriptive terms in your right-hand column than in your left. This indicates a failure in self-love, not discipline. You are not a procrastinator. Your unconscious is trying to protect itself from further abuse in the only way it knows how: by shutting down communication. Ease up on the negative self-labeling and it will feel safer about contacting you again.

CHAPTER 4

TOTE THAT BARGE, LIFT THAT BALE: The Master/Slave Relationship

In Stanley Kubrick's film of Stephen King's *The Shining,** the sentence "All work and no play, makes Jack a dull boy," typed over and over again, comprises the three-hundred-odd pages of manuscript the deranged writer Jack Torrance has pecked out in that classic retreat of blocked writers, a deserted mountain resort. It is an eloquent telegram of protest from his enslaved unconsciousness. (Later Torrance takes an axe to his family, a less wholesome form of revolt.)

Unlike most of the jobs and chores that occupy our lives, the act of creating a work of art involves the whole person. That is at once its great blessing and its curse. In the same way that clouds pass before and then uncover the sun, deep self-awareness is a state that comes and goes. The burden of the creative writer is to be sensitive much of the time to whether or not she is in touch with herself, for this state has an immediate effect on the ability to imagine something and put it down on paper. If you are out of touch with your self, it is still relatively easy to keypunch, saw wood, or tally accounts. But it is usually (though not always) very hard to write when not in a state of heightened awareness. Then comes the doodling, the forcing, the lack of concentration, the guilt—all work and no play.

The elusive and maddening nature of being in touch with yourself is simply that it is a state that cannot be *controlled* but only *allowed*. This means adjusting yourself to the creative demands of your unconscious, not the other way around, and represents self-regulation to the situation. As Fritz Perls has aptly described it:

---

*Screenplay by the critic and novelist Diane Johnson.

You don't drive a car according to a program, like, "I want to drive 65 miles per hour." You drive according to the situation. You drive a different speed at night, you drive a different speed when there is traffic there, you drive differently when you are tired. You listen to the situation. The less confident we are in ourselves, the less we are in touch with ourselves and the world, the more we want to control.

"Listening to the situation" is something a tyrant finds hard to do, intent as he or she is on asserting will at all costs. To impose on yourself an ego-conceived framework of duty, schedule, and appropriate topics of composition is an attempt to dam, channel, and otherwise divert the river of spontaneous creation in directions it does not wish to follow and in which it would not naturally flow. This invariably triggers the psychic reaction we call writer's block.

The creative experience can and must be guided, but it cannot be controlled. Control in its extreme form represents the attempt of one small segment of your psyche to declare absolute power over the rest. For it seems true, as the British writer of supernatural fiction Arthur Machen once suggested, that

> the human soul, so far from being one and indivisible, might possibly turn out to be a mere polity, a state in which dwelt many strange and incongruous citizens, whose characters were not merely unknown but altogether unsurmised by that form of consciousness which so rashly assumed that it was not only the president of the republic but also its sole citizen.

These strange fellow citizens of ours, as we all come painfully to realize in the course of a lifetime, are highly independent, egalitarian souls. They do not take kindly to dictatorship, and the forms their rebellion takes are as varied and devious as the human heart itself.

Primary among your inner cotenants is that proud being, your creative child. Every word you write is the product of a dialogue between your conscious self and your unconscious, and with every word, you move closer toward fruitful partnership or war. If it comes to war, both sides will lose. You and your creative child must cooperate or you will destroy each other as well as your common undertaking.

You have the responsibility of guiding the spontaneous uprushings of your unconscious. But the minute you try to exert excessive control on the flow of unconscious ideas, it stops, for your creative child refuses to be your slave. When this rebellion occurs, you have the choice of responding in one of various ways:

1. (This is the most common.) You entrench yourself behind your bogus authority and issue an even stricter command, trying to force obedience. "I said *create*, damn you! We'll sit here all day until you do it!" This exertion of will is not an option for chronically blocked writers, because they have typically abused the privilege with *too much* will. (In a milder form, however, it does work for those writers who rarely abuse the privilege of a command.)

2. Relax your will. Literally unclench the muscles of your mind. Take a walk, listen to music. Then, if possible, proceed with writing.

3. If your resistance persists, put aside the project for a longer period of time. Keeping your mind completely open and nonjudgmental, allow whatever doubts, hesitations, or other feelings you may be having about the work to enter consciousness. This may take a day, a week, or longer. Awareness of what is going wrong or right with your project takes its own time in emerging into consciousness, especially if you are not accustomed to listening to yourself. It will never break through at all if it encounters only a fortified stone wall.

In procedure 3, which represents one of the most vital

functions of the creative process, you may recognize our *bête noire,* procrastination, in transfigured form. Such a calculated delay has allowed the creative process to proceed undisturbed in the unconscious. The results of deliberate procrastination have been perfectly described by the artist Eugène Delacroix: "When one yields oneself completely to one's soul, it opens itself completely to one."

To the overcontrolling personality, however, this period of quiescence may prove a fruitless waste of time because such a mind is closed off to the important information about the writing process that the unconscious is trying to communicate by temporarily halting the production of words. (This state of receptivity, or active silence, will be further explored in Chapter 13.)

OUGHT VERSUS WANT

The key symptom of the controlling personality is the *oughts* and *shoulds* that crowd his or her life. "I ought to go to exercise class." "I shouldn't eat chocolate again." "I should be able to write ten pages a day." Make a list of all your most persistent *oughts* in life (see also the exercise at the end of this chapter). Note two striking characteristics of your list: (1) the severity (often unrealistic) of the expectations and (2) the glaring, inescapable truth that the things you ought to do, you *don't.* The existential truth about oughts is that we don't do them. That's why they're oughts to begin with.

This is the classic syndrome of the master-slave relationship: Any command made by your ego that the unconscious finds unpalatable, it will not perform. Period. Almost anything you set up as an ought you are doomed never to accomplish. No matter how much your ego desires it, the rest of your psyche takes perverse pleasure in denying gratification. Though the master may keep stubbornly insisting that he/she is the master, the slave refuses to be the slave.

Fritz Perls has conceptualized this personality conundrum as a split between the two parts of the psyche he calls topdog and underdog:

> The topdog usually is righteous and authoritarian; he knows best. He is sometimes right, but always righteous. The topdog is a bully, and works with "You should" and "You should not." The topdog manipulates with demands and threats of catastrophe. . . .
>
> The underdog manipulates with being defensive, apologetic, wheedling, playing the cry-baby, and such . . . the underdog is cunning, and usually gets the better of the topdog because the underdog is not as primitive as the topdog. So the topdog and underdog strive for control. Like every parent and child, they strive with each other for control. The person is fragmented into controller and controlled.
>
> This is the basis for the famous self-torture game. We usually take for granted that the topdog is right, and in many cases the topdog makes impossible perfectionistic demands. So if you are cursed with perfectionism, then you are absolutely sunk. This ideal is a yardstick which always gives you the opportunity to browbeat yourself, to berate yourself and others. Since this ideal is an impossibility, you can never live up to it.

I will return to the role of perfectionism later. Here, simply note the distortion of perfectionism into a weapon for the ego to use against the creative child. And, as Perls further observes, in any inner conflict of this sort, the underdog always wins, though not in a productive way. By sabotaging orders, the slave becomes the true master. That is why we don't stick to our diets, exercise every day, or turn out ten pages of deathless prose like clockwork every morning. We prefer thumbing our noses—or cutting them off—to following orders.

But, you point out, these particular goals are modest, healthy ones. They are not examples of impossible perfectionism; they are easily within the realm of human achievement. *Other* people achieve them, certainly; the world is full of slender people, athletic people, prolific writers. Yes, but many of these people (masochistic overachievers excluded) do what they do by preference, not command. They *like* to, and it fits their natural rhythm; no unnatural effort is required.

Make a list now of everything you love doing, that you do by preference, that you look forward to doing every day. Now examine your list. Chances are that a number of your choices—reading, for instance—are wholesome activities that many others feel they ought to do but don't.

Behind the word *ought,* then, lies a hideous tangle of autocratic attitudes and superstitions that can strangle the joy of writing. Here are some standard "oughts" the demon puts into the beginning writer's mind:

1. If I'm ever going to be famous, I ought to be writing right now.
2. I ought to write like Ernest Hemingway did, up before daybreak, standing at his desk, always stopping while he still knew what would happen next so he'd have a starting place the next day.
3. I ought to be writing every night/weekend instead of having fun.

It is easy, once they are dragged into the daylight of consciousness, to counter each of these assumptions.

1. You can only write to write, not to be famous. Expectations of future glory tend to stifle creativity. (More on this in Chapter 5.)

2. Two of these statements are certainly embellishments on the truth,* and I suspect the third of being the same. Even if they were true, beware the fallacy of the Master's Example. Every writer, by heeding his/her own deepest instincts, spins a unique web of idiosyncratic habits that make up a writing routine. At best, it's helpful to know there's so much individual variation. But what worked for Kafka is not necessarily going to work for you.

3. Do not use writing as an excuse to ruin your life.

Now, if writing is on your list of *oughts* but not *loves*, this does not necessarily mean—especially if you have already written a great deal—that your ego has shoehorned you into a profession for which you have no great avocation or love. What it probably indicates is that over the years you have moved away from your initial childlike and playful joy in writing. It is now a duty-bound and ego-ridden chore. And no activity, viewed from this perspective, is very enticing.

Perhaps you are trapped in an ego image of "author" to which you don't feel entitled (this mistake is by no means confined to amateur or unpublished writers). The very phoniness of this image, the fact that you are trying to prostitute that very private part of yourself to impress friends and the world at large, is enough to cause a temporary or permanent shutdown of your creative powers.

Most writers who have struggled through the beginning and intermediate stages of their apprenticeship, however, have had at least *some* of this inflation knocked out of them by virtue of the enormous amounts of rejection and frustration they have had to endure. What is more likely to have happened during the long struggle to gain a regular writing

*Up before daybreak and stopping while he still knew what would happen next. Hemingway was a severely blocked writer in his later years. See A.E. Hotchner, *Papa Hemingway* (New York: Random House, 1966).

rhythm is that in reaching for the brass ring of discipline you have grasped the nettle of control.

DISCIPLINE VERSUS CONTROL

We have already stressed that creative discipline is based upon spontaneous, pleasurable play, not a Spartan regime of stern self-control. From the Latin *disciplina*, meaning instruction or knowledge (a disciple is literally a "learner"), discipline is training that produces a certain pattern of behavior. The grim connotation the word has come to carry reflects more the austerity of our culture than the true nature of this enjoyable, life-enhancing experience. Discipline is not the same as forcing yourself to do distasteful tasks. Tasks, in fact, tend to become distasteful only to the degree they are forced. That we usually mistake control for discipline is a measure of our personal as well as societal rigidity. Only a writing routine that has the consent of the total psyche can provide a foundation solid enough to sustain you through the years of drudgery and tedium all creative effort requires.

How do you free discipline from the killing grip of control? Here is the therapist Muriel Schiffman's solution:

> I used to struggle anew each day with the problem, "Should I write now or later, or maybe skip this one day?" until I began to treat myself exactly as I did my small children.
>
> Now at a specific hour each morning I stop whatever I am doing and sit down at the typewriter. No need for the daily conflict between "want" and "should." . . . I write for exactly one hour each morning, no more, no less. Writing for one hour seems a natural creative activity for me. Ideas flow smoothly without stress or strain. But after an hour the work becomes an effort of will, a forced assignment, performed with much physical tension (clenched teeth, etc.), like swimming upstream.

I learned by trial and error that morning is the best time for me to write: words come easily. Later in the day I get bogged down in a compulsive search for the "perfect" word. I torture myself with inhibiting thoughts. . . .

I do not *know* why this happens in the afternoon and not in the morning. . . . My Adult self avoids frustrating the Child in me by choosing a time which is most comfortable for writing, just as it chooses the most satisfying menu when I diet. I never forced my children to eat foods they disliked just because they were "good" for them.

Muriel Schiffman established her discipline by trusting the organism, not her ego. She guided herself only to the extent of setting aside that hour to allow the writing to happen; that was her conscious self's productive input in this partnership. Her trust in her innate creative rhythms (instead of the judgmental "only *one* hour?") was rewarded by a free and uninterrupted flow of writing for the allotted period every day. And an hour a day can produce a lot of writing.

Here the Devil may tempt you with the thought: "If I do this much in an hour, think how much I could do if I worked eight hours every day!" This kind of falsely rational conclusion will only get you into trouble. Most blocked writers have a conscious expectation of results that far exceeds their unconscious preference, and the "block" is nothing more than the gap between these two opposing perspectives. The nature of our deep inner inclinations, their rhythms and direction, can be determined only by patiently *allowing* a pattern to emerge. Once the pattern has surfaced, your conscious self can step in cautiously to guide it, exploit and build on it. Each time you attempt to work faster than your inner rhythm, it will break down. That is your signal to let up and allow the unconscious once again to set the pace. You determine your limits by testing them gently but repeatedly, then respecting them—no matter how unlike anybody else's they are.

This can be a time-consuming process, even for a person who does not tend to be overcontrolling. For the blocked writer who has spent years abusing herself in a master-slave struggle, it is likely to take even longer. Freedom to develop a true discipline does not come overnight. The abused organism needs time to heal its wounds, to recover from the all-too-familiar pattern of command-rebellion-punishment and to begin to establish a new one. Such a gentle reorganization can, however, occur. And it is a far pleasanter process than whipping yourself. The key is to be able to give up pain for pleasure, and most people find this very hard to do.

Donald Newlove, a fiction writer and recovered alcoholic, recounts the agonies he experienced, blocked by ambitious plans for a nine-hundred-page novel:

> For three months I sat around my fellowship table [at Alcoholics Anonymous meetings] and complained of my fears and paralysis. . . . I'd explain carefully that my method of writing was to write a first draft in longhand, type that up, correct and retype it from start to finish, then again correct and totally retype it. Since the novel was set at NINE HUNDRED PAGES, this meant that when done I'd have filled THIRTY-SIX HUNDRED PAGES with my writing. This was daunting. The idea that I would have to fill 3600 pages with my imagination was now a black mountain of work that had kept me stoned with weakness for three months. . . .

Then came the epiphany:

> This dumb phrase suddenly filled me with light. It was: One Day at a Time. . . . To write it I had only to write one word at a time, one phrase at a time, one sentence at a time, one paragraph at a time, one page at a time, one day at a time—and if I wrote four pages a day I'd be done in three years. The magnitude of the results of this simpleminded approach to boating

my white whale sent me home like a shot after the meeting and I jumped at the dining room table with a blank sheet and began.

What Newlove has described is the conversion experience of a man who stops wanting to punish himself and starts wanting to be kind to himself. It is perhaps significant that this change occurred within a therapeutic setting.

To gain true discipline, it is necessary to learn to treat yourself with at least the same courtesy, respect, and affection you accord your spouse, friends, and even the Safeway bagboy. This sounds easy, but it is not. The urge to hate and tyrannize yourself does not go away by itself; this is what takes the *real* effort. Even in fairy tales, frogs don't change back into princes until (1) a ritual period of time (a year and a day, seven years) has passed, and (2) certain tasks have been performed. We have already seen the importance of time; the task—of gaining self-respect—is a lifework.

RESPECTING THE EGO: AN IMPORTANT NOTE

In these pages you will frequently find a villainous, punishing ego contrasted with a noble, put-upon unconscious. This distorted emphasis is necessary to right the balance between these two components of the psyche in those writers who experience themselves as blocked. Such writers have commonly attempted to dominate their unconscious instead of establishing a true relationship with it. As Cocteau said, "Art is a marriage of the conscious and unconscious"; it does not spring from an unequal relationship. Uncovering ways of relaxing this iron grip on yourself is the main purpose of this book, which attempts to suggest that the path back to writing is, by definition, effortless.

Once the imbalance is righted, however, we must recognize that the ego is an important, powerful, and positive component of the total psyche whose duty is to guide and structure the inchoate outpourings of the unconscious. The unconscious, in turn, is by no means always your "better half"; it can sweep you into a crushing depression or even psychosis. And there is sometimes a fine line, as we will see, between the spontaneous desires of the creative child and the infantile destructiveness of some unconscious impulses. Maintaining the *balance* is the crucial issue.

Let us not leave this subject without further noting that *sometimes* (blocked writers approach with caution) the only way out of an impasse is to exert the ego, not the unconscious. As Christopher Isherwood noted, "Even the tiniest act of the will towards a thing is better than not doing it at all." And tiny acts of will, as we shall see, get you where you want to go much more efficiently than great big acts of will that are hollow and unsupported by desire.

WHAT I OUGHT TO WRITE

Think of a project you have been struggling to write, with no success. Make a list of thoughts about this project. Begin each item on the list in the following manner:

    1. I *ought* to write _____ because . . .

Now write a new list.

    1. I *refuse* to write _____ because . . .

Notice that the fact that you are not able to get going on your project means that your second list of reasons is more powerful than your first. Can you learn to value your refusals consciously as much as you do unconsciously?

Now write a third list:

    1. I would love to write _____

List everything you would feel eager and enthusiastic about starting, no matter how trivial or silly your ego judges them to be. (And think about actually trying one of them, just for the fun of it.)

HOW I OUGHT TO BE—HOW I REALLY AM

Compose a dialogue between your conscious self ("I") and your unconscious (give it a separate identity and name it, if you wish). When you finish your dialogue, describe the personalities of the two speakers. What kind of person is the "I"? What kind of person is the unconscious? Are they opposites, or are they kindred spirits? Are they at loggerheads, or do they achieve resolution? (Don't try to force a resolution; that is your ego taking over. Be absolutely honest about where you are *right now*.) Rewrite this dialogue periodically to see what, if any, new twists and turns it takes.

BACK-DOOR DISCIPLINE:
LETTING THE FIELD LIE FALLOW

Resolving entrenched writer's block often means having the courage not to write for long periods of time. As long as you find that happening to you anyway, why not risk a *positive* silence for a change? Dare to aim for less and you write more, in the long run. Your long-term productivity will increase in direct proportion to the care and acceptance you lavish on your short-term silences.

Make a deliberate decision *not* to do any creative work for a one-week period. Make this an active, positive choice that leaves you free to enjoy all the rest of your life activities with no nagging guilt. (The more energy you put into enjoying the state of *not working on a project*, the more successful this exercise will be.)

At the end of your enjoyable noncreative week, take your writing pulse: Would you like to extend your grace period again, or would you like to do some writing?

Absolute honesty is essential here, for there is no "right" choice except the one you deeply incline toward. If you deeply prefer to have another week without writing, *give it to yourself* and enjoy it to the hilt. If you deeply prefer to start creative work, do so, but not on a production-quota basis.

At the end of your second week, take your pulse again: Another week of the same, or is it time to switch? Again, *either choice is right* if you are basing your decision on what you truly want to do (not on what you "ought" to do). A set amount of time when you are actively not writing allows you to build momentum and anticipation toward doing some creative work.

Many blocked writers experience the "free" week of work as an enormous relief. To choose consciously not to work increases your sense of self-mastery and decreases your self-blame, feelings of impotence, and the like. Sincerely practiced, this exercise gradually helps blur the barriers between creating and noncreating until the week of creative work becomes the holiday instead of the other way around.

CHAPTER 5

WHEN YOUR BEST IS NEVER GOOD ENOUGH: Perfectionism and Criticism

A perfect poem is impossible. Once it had been written, the world would end.

—Robert Graves

So you're a perfectionist. Does that mean, in the words of Fritz Perls, that you are "cursed, absolutely cursed"?

The answer is: yes and no. How much writing can you really do when an insidious voice is always whispering that your best is not only not good enough but awful, worthless, ridiculous? But perfectionism is a blessing as well as a curse. As a positive factor in the creative process, perfectionism is a real spur to artistic achievement and one of the vital ingredients distinguishing art from self-expression. Without the slightly obsessive, controlling urge to excel, artists do not have that fine cutting edge, that need to *make completely* (the literal meaning of "perfect"), which produces all real works of art.

In other words, do not stand the master-slave relationship on its head and scold yourself for a desire to be perfect in your writing. That impulse is just as natural a part of the creative process as postponement is.

Past a certain point of healthy obsession, however, the impetus to shape and perfect reverses itself and becomes negative. You know you have crossed the border from persistence to paralysis when every fragile word or idea withers under the glare of disapproval and faultfinding from your demonic Judge. And here again you will usually find that willpower ("the power of positive thinking") is a pitifully weak defense in the face of the Judge's relentless ferocity. Pepping yourself up with phony defensive compliments ("But I *am* a good writer") is exhausting and not much help, either. After a token bit of effort, you usually collapse into grim and acquiescent silence.

In this case, writer's block becomes an automatic defense against baring yourself to the unending insults of a merciless inner Judge. Unless you can find a way to silence that critical voice, it literally isn't *safe* to write, for no sane person voluntarily subjects herself to that kind of abuse. Your writer's block will continue to function as protection from your own self-hatred until you find a way, not to bulldoze through the block, but to defuse the hatred.

How, exactly, is this done?

Before we examine the possibilities, two interesting variations on the perfectionist phenomenon need to be mentioned. One of these might be termed "fear of perfection," that is, breaking off in the middle of your effort because you have started so well, so flawlessly, that you are afraid (no, you *know*) you are incapable of carrying the whole thing off at the same level. A friend and colleague, William Searle, recalls how, as a first grader in 1943-1944 during the height of World War II, he and his classmates obsessively drew military airplanes. The rules regarding identification of these planes were strict: Handsome airplanes were American; "scrubby and mean-looking" planes were German or Japanese and were generally set on fire as an added touch. These conventions posed a real aesthetic challenge, because it was harder to bring off an American plane successfully and "flames had the advantage of being comparatively easy to draw." Ultimately one boy found himself in a classic dilemma:

> Though relatively untalented, he had managed by a fluke to draw the nose, wings, and most of the fuselage of as beautiful an aircraft as I had ever seen. . . . it was too large, sleek and elegant-looking to be anything convincingly but American— there was nothing for it but to draw stars. Should he try to finish it at the risk of spoiling it? or set it on fire?

Searle's classmate chose the easy way out. Instead of finishing it, he torched the American airplane, a decision that outraged his fellow students as much for aesthetic reasons as for patriotic ones.

My own sympathies are completely with that first grader who, through no fault of his own, was suddenly propelled down the inexorable and unforgiving road of perfectionism. So what if he committed a sin against Art? No one who has ever set fire to a story or poem out of sheer failure of nerve can fail to appreciate his point of view. The spectacle of naked excellence can be frightening, even repelling, and one's strongest impulse is sometimes to say, "Torch it, for God's sake!" On this principle Moslem weavers always include a deliberate error in the pattern of their rugs to avoid offense in the sight of God, the only entity able to encompass perfection.

Imperfection also has its own inscrutable advantages. The English novelist Penelope Farmer tells the story of a school competition for the best picture of a party. The prize-winning drawing showed an empty room, a table piled high with festive goodies and, in the background, a single hand, emerging from behind a slightly open door. Asked about her inspiration for this magnificently evocative scene, the child artist replied that she had to do it that way because she couldn't draw people.

For literary history's most famous case of a work immolated in midcomposition, we must turn to Samuel Taylor Coleridge's poem "Kubla Khan." His transparent excuse of a "person from Porlock" who happened to interrupt the sacred trance of poetic concentration, together with the cynical responses of later poets, is a major document in the annals of writer's block. See the Appendix.

The second variant of the perfectionist block might be called the "reverse Midas effect." This happens after you have finished a preliminary draft and reread it only to discover that an amazing transformation has occurred: What you thought was pure gold in the throes of composition has turned into something brown and odorous. The resulting effect on your pride is so devastating that you either throw it away or embark on an ill-advised course of drastic and usually fatal revision. Curiously, reading the offending piece a third time, you may find it neither good nor bad, for attitudes toward one's own work constantly shift and change.

In all three versions of the perfectionist block, it is clear that habitual and severe faultfinding is a problem of the *personality*, the whole human being, not of artistic technique. Excessive perfectionism is self-hatred in still another mask.

THE INTERNAL JUDGE

> *The perfectionists . . . finding or believing life to be intolerable except for art's perfection, by the very violence of their homage can render art imperfect.*
> —*Cyril Connolly*

Now let's watch how perfectionism becomes the tool of self-hatred. A sample dialogue between you and your inner Judge might go something like this:

YOU: (*Write, write, write.*)
JUDGE: Stop! That's terrible.
YOU (*stopping*): What?
JUDGE: What you just wrote. It stinks. "He put the cards on the table in the back room."
YOU: What's wrong with that?
JUDGE: "On the table in the back room." Don't put two prepositional phrases in a row like that. Don't you know any better?

Now that your Judge, and not your writing, has your full attention, what are you going to do? Consider two possible responses:

CAVE-IN: Oh, gee. Let's see—"He put the cards on the back room table." "Going into the back room, he put the cards—" (*Concentration and overall train of thought now totally lost.*)
BETTER: Shut up. I'll take care of that *if* I think it needs taking care of, when I rewrite. Quit interrupting.

Some people, of course, compose in such a way that they cannot proceed to the next word until the present word is exactly as it should be. In their case, the Judge is not an obstacle but part of a tried-and-true modus operandi; they are completely adapted to his presence. In many writers, however, this carping voice, as an interrupter of spontaneous performance, has the effect of tripping you in midstride and, if mistakenly heeded, can effectively shut down a day's work. The Judge has no place in first-draft composition.

This is a slightly different interaction from that seen in the master-slave relationship underlying most chronic writer's block. Here your unconscious negativity is the master, and you, your conscious self, are the slave; your own self-contempt is acting upon you almost as an impersonal force. The entrenched negativity of an inner Judge poses a serious danger, and new tactics are needed. Self-insult must be stopped at the source; you have to face the bully down. This time you are the beleaguered slave who must overthrow the tyrant; you must refuse to accept those lies. When the voice begins, you must tell it in no uncertain terms to stop. And it will know whether or not you're bluffing.

How do you say no with conviction to the bully? How do you summon true authority? There is no end of excellent reasons you can call upon, of course—for example, that obsessive perfectionism is stifling, life-denying, and ultimately a dull and unadventuresome method of self-laceration. These reasons are not likely to make an impression. The real way to put conviction in your voice is to realize that you are facing a life-or-death situation. This encounter with your self-hatred is potentially as dangerous as being accosted by a crazed gunman, a special kind of madman who will spare you if you oppose and reject him, but will almost certainly kill you if you give in. To cave in to excessive self-criticism, to surrender yourself along with all you have struggled so hard to create, is to allow your personhood to be violated at the deepest level. Over a lifetime, unfortunately, such a series of meek surrenders can become just as addicting a habit as alcohol.

To say no to self-denigration, then, involves a commitment of the whole spirit to believe in yourself and take seriously what you are doing. It cannot be a shallow behavior-modification exercise in which, as the theory goes, if you say the magic word enough times, you come to believe in it. In this case, you must believe in it completely *before* you can say it with sufficient strength to silence the torrent of abuse.

Silencing the inner Judge when he goes too far does not mean that everything you write will be wonderful, or that someday you will not pick up something you wrote and discover that it really *was* trite and worthless after all. The act of writing does not in itself guarantee the production of art. All you are really doing is buying yourself time and freedom—to write first, perfect later.

There is still another critic to deal with, one you are not equipped to face until you have come to some kind of terms with your internal enemy. What is this new critic? Your audience: every soul out there who reads your work and feels compelled to comment on it.

THE EXTERNAL JUDGE:
SHOWING YOUR WORK TO OTHERS

Most writers, in the course of their careers, become
thick-skinned and learn to accept vituperation, which
in any other profession would be unimaginably offen-
sive, as a healthy counterpoise to praise.

—Evelyn Waugh

External judges—that is, your readers—are potentially capable of a truly disinterested dislike of your work. Their lack
of enthusiasm has an objective reality that you cannot order
away or dissipate by three days' fasting on the mountaintop;
you must learn to live with it just as much as you must learn
to live with their praise, which can cause problems of its
own.

Criticism of your work by others, depending on whether it is favorable or unfavorable, is likely to have one of two
undesirable effects: It will *inflate* you, or it will *deflate* you.
Neither condition is suitable for writing, and each can take its
own special toll on your work. This is as true of the seasoned
professional reading a bad (or good) review in a national
magazine as it is of the beginner showing his first effort to his
college roommate.

Let's examine the process from the beginning, the moment when you first hand a manuscript to anyone other than
your mother to read. At this point, it is wise to remember two
important considerations:

1. Manuscript reading is an art apart from ordinary
reading. Unless the person you have given your work to is an
experienced and sensitive professional, your typed page will
lack for him the authority of the printed page or the bound
volume. For most people outside publishing (as well as for
many inside), a typed manuscript subliminally signals "amateur." Consequently, they tend to find flaws in it they

wouldn't perceive in the same piece if it were published in *Esquire*.

2. Whether your reader is a professional or a nonprofessional, there is always the all-important question of *taste*. Not all people like the same things, nor for the same reasons. Above a certain level of technical competence, one person's Shakespeare is another's hack; you begin to realize this only after a great many people have read and commented on your work. Some people will like your work even if it is very bad; others will hate it even if it is very good. There are people utterly wrong about your work who are heartbreakingly persuasive in their reasons; there are completely inarticulate people who intuitively sense what your work is all about.

This is the maddening, elusive nature of criticism: We want it to be an absolute, and it is not. It never is. How do you distinguish valid from invalid criticism? Determining whether it is valid and what, if anything, you can do about it is one of the most difficult tasks of the writing experience. In fact, it is often impossible. We are as blind to most of the effects our works have on others as we are to the impression our personalities make. There are a thousand ways to rationalize away someone's negative reception of your work, against the single haunting (and usually far more compelling) possibility that the critic may be right on target.

In the final analysis, you must rely on your own deepest inner convictions about your work. Does the information you are receiving from the outside resonate with what you are feeling inside? If so, it may be worth doing something about. Tuning into relevant criticism and tuning out the irrelevant becomes a delicate matter of sorting the seeds, slowly and painstakingly. Needless to say, this fine task of discrimination is virtually impossible to accomplish if a domineering inner Judge is constantly running radio interference or agreeing eagerly with the worst criticism.

If you are wincing under the sting of negative feedback

from others, a block will rise up between you and your writing as a radical measure to protect you from further abuse (if you don't write anything at all, how can you be criticized?). This is a self-protective reaction of the organism; when your wounds have healed sufficiently, you will in most cases be able to continue. Those who are almost permanently crippled after a bad review must ask themselves why. Have they allowed the voices of their critics to form an unholy chorus with their own internal demon, thereby providing a spurious justification for self-hatred?

Every writer is, in his or her own way, terribly vulnerable. This being the case, should you show your work to anyone at all besides those responsible for getting it published? This depends entirely on you and your assessment of how defenseless you really are. Cynthia Ozick has stated: "Writers have a little holy light within, like a pilot light, which fear is always blowing out. When a writer brings a manuscript fresh from the making, at the moment of greatest vulnerability, that's the moment for friends to help get the little holy light lit again."

The encouragement friends or other writers give may help create a benign, accepting environment in which your writing can flourish—if you are clever enough to find readers who always like your work. Beware of the beginner's error of assuming that just because your reader is another writer, he or she will *ipso facto* be sympathetic to your intentions. In many cases, the reverse is true: Writers who are passionately attached to their own ways of rendering art may be far less objective or even insightful than other readers.

Protect yourself, or expose yourself, in any way your instinct feels is right. You will have to determine by trial and considerable error whether this means showing your work to anyone who will read it or showing it to no one but your agent and/or editor. If you are just starting out and feel extremely tentative, it is perfectly acceptable to spend years accreting your work in the dark; many writers begin in this way. But it is a big mean world out there, and further down the road a case can be made (if you are truly ready for it) for the *tempering* effects rejection and adverse criticism can have on your own nature as well as on your work. As we like to say about any thoroughly unpleasant experience, it builds character.

How can you distinguish valid negative criticism from the invalid if you have never experienced either? You are likely to be crushed by the latter, when it inevitably comes, if you have not had some experience of all kinds of reactions and thus have learned how to define yourself independently from them.

On the other hand, praise, which we naturally (but mistakenly) feel no need to defend ourselves against, can be just as insidious as rejection—*and it is no more likely to be true* (the chances that it is are about fifty-fifty). Its inflationary effects can remove you just as far from your real self as a bad notice can. Unlike bad press, however, praise is something you can rapidly become dependent on. When fickle tastes inevitably change, the previously cosseted writer is likely to be more devastated than the poor soul who has continued to struggle along under steady fire or against sheer indifference. If you rely on praise to keep afloat, what happens when critics decide you're no good? You may go down with the ship. When the English writer Barbara Pym's eighth novel was arbitrarily turned down by the publisher of her first seven, she was unable to write a line for the next sixteen years. This sensitive writer accepted a short-sighted "market" decision as a true judgment of her worth.

It is a truism of creative endeavor that praise in the early stages is always beneficent. The poet Diane Wakoski, however, makes an interesting case against automatic approval, especially in the setting that has become the traditional launching pad of young American writers, namely, the creative writing class:

> The workshop system produces what I call workshop junkies: people who do not become original writers because they continue to be encouraged for everything they do. They get so used to and so needful of that encouragement that they never want to go out in the world and struggle with that feeling of aloneness: "No one ever reads me. What does my work mean? I've written for 50 years and it hasn't done anything to change the world." Or, "I've spent all my time doing this and I'm not even satisfied with it." Those are all the feelings that even a great writer has. . . . The workshop . . . allows [the student] to think that he's already a poet before he's even written 15 or 50 or 150 poems.

In too large doses, praise can have a paralyzing effect on your work in the form of a block: A piece that has garnered accolades can become an impossibly hard act to follow. A young writer's overpraised first novel and his corresponding inflation, for example, can combine to produce a toxic environment for further creative efforts.

Either way, letting the opinions of others define your work gives them far too much power over your artistic identity. Paradoxically, lack of interest in or outright dislike of your writing, if you can keep it from overwhelming you, can work more to your advantage than an enthusiastic and uncritical reception. An atmosphere of benign neglect can give you the freedom to grow as a writer; an atmosphere of outright disapproval, if you survive it (as all writers must, at some time), can temper you as a person, giving your inner self that Zen-like equilibrium that remains unchanged in the face of good fortune or bad. In time, this inner resilience gradually supplants the more primitive mechanism of writer's block as the protector of your selfhood and the integrity of your work. Then inner and outer Judges become guides pointing out direction that you, the final judge and arbiter, may or may not choose to follow, according to your deepest preference.

MOMENT OF TRUTH

Your work is about to be published or critiqued and you expect to receive feedback in the form of reviews, evaluations, and so forth. Before your work "goes public," take a quiet moment by yourself and write a review of your own, *in the third person* (for the sake of distancing):

> Mary B's novel is a bundle of paradoxes. On one hand it—etc.

As if you were an objective reviewer, explain the purpose or intent of your work and (most important) what is strongest and weakest in it. Be as detailed as you like. Be totally honest in your evaluation.

You now have written a document of your own with which to compare the reactions of others. If Editor X in fact does not like your work, *you do not have to identify wholly with his criticisms;* you have already defined your own position as distinct from his. Some of his strictures you may want to accept, others reject; some will come as a complete surprise. With your review, however, you are at least able to keep his viewpoint separate from your own.

Conversely, if Critic Y thinks you are the absolute greatest, some of your own recorded reservations about your work can help keep you from experiencing a dangerous inflation. (Remember: The wrong kind of praise can be as lethal as a pan.)

CHAPTER 6

GREAT EXPECTATIONS: Excessive Ambition

[Ross Lockridge] talked about his book without a pause. He explained that he and William Shakespeare had solved a particular dramatic problem in the same fashion and guessed that in two hundred years' time readers would still be discussing the symbolism of Raintree County, *His amazed audience looked for some sign of jest, or the chance to join the conversation, in vain.*

—John Leggett, *Ross and Tom*

There is an almost mathematical ratio between soaring, grandiose ambition, when it is not firmly anchored in the daily trivia of production, and a severe creative block. Norman Mailer, who once declared that he would "try to hit the longest ball ever to go up into the accelerated air of our American letters," never got around to writing the opus—*Ancient Evenings*, one suspects, was not the work originally announced—though bulletins of its imminent appearance have been issued by the author over the twenty-odd years since he made his proud boast. Ross Lockridge, unable to begin a new book and plagued by severe depression, took his own life shortly after the publication of *Raintree County*.

One might expect overambition to be a beginner's problem, teenage daydreaming of the sort everyone loves to indulge in, that will drop away after years of humbling labor, when you realize just what an enormous amount of work (not merely that overrated commodity, talent) stands between you and Tolstoi et al. But this is not the case. There are countless well-known authors whose lust for greatness throbs in every line, ruining what natural grace their work possesses with the self-consciousness that comes from pathological ambition—and these writers are also often severely blocked.

Still, fantasies of grandeur are more likely to form when your mode of self-expression is not yet clearly defined and you seek to align yourself with the masters. The achievement of past literary giants can certainly serve as inspiration, but to reach those snowy peaks in the distance requires fifty years of painfully slow backpacking, one foot after the other. And when you get to the end of the trail, wherever that happens to be, your journey will turn out to have been entirely different from anyone else's before or since—just as each of those artists simply took the path deeper into themselves to a uniquely private destination.

It is only human nature, however, to want quick results, to try to find a shortcut through the whole tedious process of producing excellent writing. Why can't you be as great as Tolstoi *now?* Well, a voice whispers from within, maybe you *are.* Maybe this very sentence you are in the act of composing will someday be memorized by schoolchildren and—

Suddenly the act of creation comes to a grinding halt. What has happened? The contact with the deeper stratum of your self that the creative act requires has just been rudely broken by radio interference from the shrill voice of that ham operator, your ego. As we saw in Chapter 4, when the ego abandons partnership and attempts to wrest control from the unconscious, the block springs up, impenetrable. Your creative child has stuck its foot firmly in front of your "vaulting ambition, which o'erleaps itself," and you have fallen flat on your face.

Self-consciousness of any sort, but especially of the prematurely self-congratulatory sort, is death to spontaneous performance, whether you are pole-vaulting or writing a poem. Katherine Mansfield, who took the ethics of artistic creation very seriously, once noted:

> I wonder why it should be so difficult to be humble. I do not think I am a good writer; I realize my faults better than anyone else could realize them. . . . And yet, when I have finished a story and before I have begun another, I catch myself *preening* my feathers. It is disheartening. There seems to be some bad old pride in my heart; a root of it that puts out a thick shoot on the slightest provocation. . . . This interferes very much with work. One can't be calm, clear, good as one must be, while it goes on. . . . It's a kind of excitement

within one, which shouldn't be there. . . . And anything that I write in this mood will be no good; it will be full of *sediment*.

Though there is a difference in degree between the mood Mansfield is describing and the excesses quoted at the beginning of this chapter, it is actually the same thing: the state of inflation, just as pernicious to the writer as that of self-loathing.

But isn't it natural to feel pleasure from accomplishment, and beyond that, satisfaction, even love, of one's work and the desire to be recognized for what one has done? Isn't this the true antidote to the self-hate that throttles so much creativity? What can be wrong with the urge to excel, to aim high and be the best one can, to have one's work read and appreciated by the widest possible audience?

Undeniably, ambition and belief in one's future prospects play a vital, positive role in most writers' careers. Without the inner conviction of talent and worth, one could not have the strength to endure the endless rejections, insults, bad reviews, and corkscrew twists and turns of a profession in which, more than any other, advancement depends almost entirely on the judgment (often whim) of others—editors, critics, readers. And it is not just a matter of having a favorable opinion of your own talents. I question whether there has ever been a writer or any other artist who hasn't cherished the secret conviction that he or she, like Muhammad Ali—and never mind Shakespeare—is the Greatest.

Take, for example, the sculptor Benjamin Haydon, friend of John Keats, as described by Keat's biographer Aileen Ward:

> What [Haydon] described in his journals as "irresistible, perpetual, continued urgings of future greatness" used to shoot through him with such intensity that he could only "lift up his heart and thank God" for these assurances of divine favour.

Or another Romantic example, our old friend Coleridge, as described by his friend Davy:

> His will is probably less than ever commensurate with his ability. Brilliant images of greatness float upon his mind . . . agitated by every breeze, and modified by every sunbeam. He talked, in the course of one hour, of beginning three works, and he recited the poem of *Christabel,* unfinished, as I had before heard it.

Coleridge's *Biographia Literaria,* like his modern counterpart Norman Mailer's *Advertisements for Myself,* makes instructive reading not only as a potpourri of shrewd literary judgments but as self-exposure on the grand scale, a classic combination of intense vulnerability and panic-stricken self-aggrandizement of the sort often found in the writer blocked by excessive ambition.

But for every Mailer or Coleridge who will shout it to the world, thousands of more circumspect writers whisper the same sweet words in the privacy of their own souls. And if we all do it, then where's the harm?

The key, as in so many other areas of creativity, lies in moderation—especially in not daydreaming on the job. Writer's block occurs as a healthy check only to an *intrusive and persistent ambition that exceeds your present abilities by too great an order of magnitude.* You stare at the page, hypnotized, as the voice within you composes not the story you are writing, but the rave reviews it will receive upon its appearance in *The New Yorker.* Such grandiosity will kill you at the start or any other time.

Everyone has somewhere in his life "The Book," usually unfinished, never so much a real project as a container barge loaded down with a heavy cargo of ambition. Some of these books do get completed, and many are published— usually those of already established authors who are writing backward from the favorable reviews of their last books. Conceived in a state of inflation, these curiously dead works (full of the "sediment" Mansfield mentions) leave the reader feeling both uneasy and unsatisfied. They are forced, rigid, unreal.

The way out of this dead-end alley is to forget yourself, surrender your intrusive ego to your work. You must junk the Nobel Prize speech for the time being, return your eyes to the paper, and begin writing as well as you can, period.

What if the outrageous visions of future greatness persist? And what—here comes the seductive voice again—if they are prescient, totally justified? What if they should come true in the end? James Joyce, for example, declared early on, through his mouthpiece Stephen Dedalus, that he was going to "forge in the smithy of my soul the uncreated conscience of my race"—a highly impressive statement of intent. With the writing of *Ulysses*, the grandiose announcement was apparently fulfilled. It took Joyce ten years to write this book and the rest of his life (another seventeen years) to complete *Finnegans Wake**, but write them he did. Wasn't he then justified in having these dreams of future accomplishment, and even boldly proclaiming them to the world? Haven't many great artists, such as Wagner and Picasso, been monsters of egocentricity? What, in fact, is the difference between healthy ambition and destructive grandiosity?

The answer can best be found in an investigation of the gray area lying between a balanced individual's confidence in himself, his hopes and dreams, and the personality disorder of extreme egotism or narcissism, a dis-ease of the soul not to be mistaken for simple selfishness or self-absorption (both fairly common traits in writers of all sorts). Narcissism, in the nonspecialist meaning I give it here (what one writer has aptly dubbed "ego-ridden powerlessness"), is a

---

*Some heretics consider this an inflated work.

malady to which we all occasionally succumb, but only in a few does it persist past all cure.

THE FALSE MUSE NARCISSUS

The ego is the caricature people mistake for the self, the ego is the fraud, the actor, the transvestite of the self.

—*Anaïs Nin*

Blocks are simply forms of egotism.

—*Lawrence Durrell*

He had a very high opinion of himself. Sometimes it made him look like a pygmy.

—*Stanislaw Jerzy Lec*

It may seem a paradox that paralyzing ambition is a function of an unnaturally inflated ego. If self-hatred destroys creativity, wouldn't an egotistical person necessarily have a higher opinion of himself than ordinary mortals? Wouldn't he therefore be in ample possession of the self-love and self-acceptance so critical to the creative act?

The answer is no. The truth is that a "big ego" conceals a deep and overriding sense of worthlessness just as the seemingly hang-loose habit of "procrastination" hides a rule-bound compulsive personality. The egotism has formed as a *compensation,* a kind of daily self-armoring against an unbearable inner feeling of self-loathing. Egotism is a mask of superiority designed to hide—as much from its owner, significantly, as from others—the true face, inferiority. Lacking a center, the egotistical personality swings wildly between the twin psychic poles of grandiosity and utter self-contempt.

In this context, worship of the self is a kind of pathetic psychic cargo cult that fools no one, least of all the worshiper himself. The nature of any psychological compensation is that it can never truly *satisfy;* it is only a substitute—in this case, for genuine self-respect. Soon the inferiority begins to reassert its dominance. And the more insistent the feelings of worthlessness, the more frantic the attempts of the ego become to repress them. The energy the organism must expend in continuing this cover-up is excessive and debilitating. It leaves little time for any other meaningful activity, least of all creative work, which demands steady self-affirmation.

Here again, writer's block has the potential, usually not properly heeded, of working positive, healing effects on a psyche headed for narcissistic entropy. By halting the creative act the block asserts that the emperor has no clothes. By stripping off the mask of false vanity, it provides the suffering writer a clue that she should be examining herself at a deeper level than that of pipe dreams. But such an examination is just what the narcissistic personality knows it must avoid at all costs, because it means touching the psychic equivalent of an open wound. Probing the deeper level means that the inadmissible secret sense of inferiority would have to be faced. So most often the writer's attention is quickly displaced from the seesawing self-esteem to the block itself, which is then blamed for all subsequent problems. Meanwhile, the less work accomplished, the larger the fantasies become. The projected opus will not merely be good, it will be the greatest accomplishment of the century—of all recorded time. And so on.

But all fantasies require some fuel to keep them going. And when none is forthcoming in reality, artificial measures must be taken to sustain the false system. The classic shortcut for bridging the gap between excessive ambition and unrealized accomplishment is alcohol (or drugs), which keeps the ego euphoric and unnaturally inflated.

Narcissism and Alcohol: The Missing Link

*This cunning disease offers feelings of instant success
and riotous fame to one who lusts after them.*

—Donald Newlove

*Drunkenness is a substitute for art; it is in itself a low
form of creation.*

—Cyril Connolly

We all enjoy mood enhancers because they make us feel good
in a special way: They erase our usual inhibitions and open
the door to the unconscious. But there is always the danger
that one will gradually become fixed on the means, not the
end, feeling unable to contact the unconscious in any other
way. Then brief euphoria leads ever deeper into immense despair. (One of the most moving descriptions of this psychological Gordian knot can be found in Charles Jackson's *The
Lost Weekend,* a classic American novel now half forgotten.)

For every would-be writer who is an alcoholic or a drug
user, there is someone who was once a writer but is now an
alcoholic or an addict. Dependence on a substance is a full-
time occupation, and no one writes well while chronically
drunk or stoned.

Though there are many theories—psychological, bio-
chemical, even genetic—about the genesis of alcoholism
and addiction generally, a childish egotism that stubbornly
refuses to mature with physical aging is often a symptom of
this mysterious disorder. After all, what other medium than
alcohol or drugs better preserves and magnifies the characteristic adolescent mood swings between elation and despair?

In *Those Drinking Days,* a classic account of a writing/
drinking symbiosis, Donald Newlove states that he justified
his habits by the fact that "all the American writers and poets
I admired drank as I did . . . . I took all their manias and ul-

cers as badges of glory." The romantic linkage of art with alcohol was destroyed for him only after years of painful reha-
bilitation: "That the greatest writing is made out of loneli-
ness and despair magnified by booze is an idea for arrested
adolescents."

But is there any truth at all to the popular notion that an
essential link exists between genius and self-destruction? Let
us examine this tenet more closely, for it can exert a lethal influence on an impressionable and sensitive person who happens also to be a writer.

The Myth of the Suffering Genius

We all grew up with Romance in our heads
The Romance that the secret of success
Was genius, blazing gifts lighting the world.
Genius, the noble individual
Long-haired, peculiar and long suffering,
A kind of Christ, in fact, or Fisher-King . . .
—Delmore Schwartz

How [can] a genius be happy, normal—above all,
long-lived?
—Charles Jackson, The Lost Weekend

The aura of "genius" that hangs over literary endeavors like
a poison cloud is intimately related to the problem of egotism. What is a genius? A genius is somebody whose special
gifts and/or talents place him or her above the rest of the
world and its petty cares. Therefore, special treatment must
be afforded the genius because of these gifts and the sensitivity that, it is assumed, tortures him/her daily. (This reasoning
is also a handy club for keeping spouses and lovers of the
Sensitive One in line.)

A concomitant line of thought—and here is the link to alcoholism—is that geniuses, besides being sensitive and having special gifts, are tortured, self-destructive souls who take to drink, drugs, and ultimately suicide to find relief from the existential *Angst* of being artists. In any other profession, it would seem self-evident that alcoholism or madness would be a minus, not a plus, but the arts have been infected by a curious romanticism on the subject. As Newlove remarks, "You might as well say about a Bronx housewife on the sauce that the warmth she longs for has been exiled to the outer edges of life in the America of her time, it's that empty an alibi."

What is the source of this gross misapprehension about the way art is made and about the people who make it? A century and a half ago. Charles Lamb speculated in his essay "Sanity of True Genius":

> The ground of the mistake is, that men, finding in the raptures of the higher poetry a condition of exaltation to which they have no parallel in their own experience, besides the spurious resemblance of it in dreams and fevers, impute a state of dreaminess and fever to the poet. But the true poet dreams being awake. He is not possessed by his subject, but has dominion over it.

The logical extension of Lamb's thesis is Gustave Flaubert's self-command, never yet equaled for its succinctness and good sense: "Be regular and orderly in your life like a bourgeois, so that you may be violent and original in your work."

This kind of common sense does not fit conveniently with the sentimental notion of the artist's tragic lot to which chronic writer's block makes such a perfect accessory. A writer who can't write—what, after all, could be more tragic than that? Now, it can be safely said that life, for everyone, contains a strong tragic vein, but the true suffering of the artist lies in enduring the daily anxiety and tedium of "turning sentences around," of living through the unbearably slow development of his or her abilities.

There are many sensitive people who suffer terribly, but not all or most or even half of them are artists. Those artists who, *as humans,* are saddled with the terrible afflictions of mental illness or alcoholism create their work *in spite of* their infirmities, not because of them. That prosaic struggle, not the romantic patina of their disabilities, holds the true potential for heroism. Franz Kafka created great works of art in spite of his self-hatred, not because of it. By making his inner struggles the raw material of his art, he achieved a great victory over them.

Still, you say, what about Poet X and Writer Y, or dozens upon dozens of others? How do we account for the sheer number of writers who have succumbed to alcoholism, madness, or suicide? Doesn't that prove there is a connection between art and self-destruction?

The subject is too complex for full consideration here, but a correlation does seem to exist between a sheltered, intense childhood environment and a propensity for artistic expression, with self-absorption and childlike behavior persisting through adulthood. Some artists, in fact, seem to enjoy *long*—lifelong—childhoods, a quality that promotes the close and ongoing relationship with the unconscious.

There is, however, a distinction between child*like* and child*ish.* Submitting your talent to a long, exacting training, maintaining and carrying it through to fulfillment, is an extremely adult undertaking requiring a very different inner orientation than the childish egotism arising from inferiority feelings. Narcissism is a problem of personality that must be dealt with on human terms, not rationalized as the badge of genius. To paraphrase John Stuart Mill, we are men and women first, artists second. To grow as a writer, you must first grow as a person.

True works of art do not spring from a desire to be famous; they grow out of a deeper stratum of emotional and spiritual resources within the human being. Keats, struggling with his long-delayed, chronically blocked *Hyperion*, was urged by his friend Haydon, the previously mentioned narcissist, to finish the poem regardless. In reply, Keats

> announced to Haydon . . . that he had resolved "never to write for the sake of writing, or making a poem." . . . [T]he more Keats struggled with his poem, the more he realized that great poetry could not be written out of mere great ambition or even some gift of noble language, but only out of a knowledge of life which he had not yet achieved.

Keats's block represented the deeper knowledge of his unconscious that his abilities and experience were not yet on a par with his high intentions for the poem. Countless other writers as well have had to set aside their Towering Achievements and turn to more accessible channels for their talent. The opposite of inflation is small, steady steps during which ego is subordinated to work. Less is more. Aim lower and you may hit the target.

LESS IS MORE

Identify that unfinished (or finished) project of yours that was sabotaged by ambition—the one with the lyrical last (or first) paragraph that makes your eyes mist when you re-read it (this paragraph always gets written, even if the rest of the book doesn't). Compare it to some more modest effort in which your reach did not exceed your grasp. Which seems alive, which dead?

Is there any way of returning to the large project with lowered expectations and the idea of finishing or refining it in a modest, focused spirit? Or is it time, finally, to let go (see Chapter 9)?

CHAPTER 7

DIVINE CHILD, PROFANE ADULT:
The Myth of Unlimited Possibilities

Many writers and would-be writers experience chronic block not simply out of grandiose expectations but also from an overwhelming vagueness about what they are actually *able* to do, as opposed to what they might someday do, if they get around to it.

Naturally enough, the best way to maintain this comforting ignorance of one's true creative limits is by doing nothing and imagining everything. Actually to put words to paper is to abandon the divine world of the possible and enter the mundane world of trivial limitations. To take action, to write, means turning one's back on the never-never land of adolescence, where anything and everything is always about to happen, could happen, but usually never quite *does* happen.

The poet Wendell Berry has identified not one but two creative muses: the Muse of Inspiration and the Muse of Realization. This chapter will explore the psychological set of those "potential" writers who never quite get from the temple of Muse No. 1 to that of Muse No. 2, a condition that might be called the daydreaming block.

Daydreaming and fantasizing are absolutely necessary to the creative process; in fact, they make up the precreative experience, the incubation period of art. But images in your mind are nothing in themselves; they must be made manifest to be considered art. If fantasizing is prolonged indefinitely, the person floats in a diffuse and generalized dreaminess that never finds a focus or expression in art.

The number of potential writers who never succeed in breaking out of this comfortable nest of dreams is legion. Typically, the person is a talented beginner who writes scraps and fragments of stories, poems, or screenplays but is unable to develop or finish his ideas. The projected work is often a vehicle for fantasies of grandeur associated with its future reception by the world. Since to complete the work would make it only too clear whether one had really produced the Great American Novel, the would-be writer's only recourse in protecting his narcissism is to leave everything he starts unfinished so that he can sustain his fantasies. Here the creative child has been co-opted into the lesser service of immature vanity. When the unconscious is kept constantly busy churning out daydreams of glory, there is nothing left over to produce a sustained work of imagination.

A related, though not totally similar, phenomenon occurs in the university setting when countless graduate students, after a leisurely five- to ten-year course of study, find themselves unable to write their dissertations. The field must be revisited, more books must be read, related avenues of inquiry must be pursued. Why all the delaying tactics? Because no initiation rite in modern American life is more shockingly abrupt than giving up the casual delights of student life and entering the structured adult world of duties, restrictions on personal freedom, and hard tests of one's abilities and work. Understandably, people balk at the prospect of this drastic change of habits. Thus we have "thesis block," a time-honored (though usually completely unconscious) means of prolonging a carefree extended childhood as well as avoiding long-buried feelings of inadequacy.

The reluctance to leave the world of imagined future prospects for the world of real acts constitutes a kind of existential stage fright at the threshold of life. One is never quite ready to make an entrance because that means that finally one would have to commit oneself to playing a single role and no other. One lives one's possibilities in the imagination because one is afraid to test them in the outside world. As the Czech author Milan Kundera says of one of his characters:

[T]he more he suffers from the fear of trying for something
modest and well defined, the more he wants to conquer the
world, the infinity of the undefined, the indefinedness of the
infinite.

Over a lifetime, this almost universally experienced phenomenon of adolescence can harden into a permanent pos-
ture as the Hamletesque split between *posse* and *esse* widens
into a chasm.

The inability to give up the world of the possible for
the world of the actual has been labeled the *puer aeternus*
("eternal youth") syndrome by the Jungian analyst Marie
Louise von Franz, whose lectures on the subject were first
published in the United States in the mid-1970s. According
to von Franz, the typical *puer aeternus* (or *puella aeterna;* an
equal number of women manifest these symptoms)
embodies

a form of neurosis which H. G. Baynes has described as the
"provisional life," that is, the strange attitude and feeling that
one is *not yet* in real life. For the time being one is doing this
or that, but whether it is a woman or a job, it is *not yet* what is
really wanted, and there is always the fantasy that sometime
in the future the real thing will come about. If this attitude is
prolonged, it means a constant inner refusal to commit oneself to the moment. With this there is often, to a smaller or
greater extent, a savior complex, or a Messiah complex, with
the secret thought that one day one will be able to save the
world; the last word in philosophy, or religion, or politics, or
art, or something else, will be found. . . . The one thing
dreaded throughout by such a type of man is to be bound to
anything whatever. There is a terrific fear of being pinned
down, of entering space and time completely, and of being
the one human being that one is.

The extreme examples of *pueri* and *puellae* are familiar enough and even possess a certain severe beauty of form: the fifty-year-old Santa Monica surfer with skin like a crocodile's; the golden hippie now hardening into middle-aged street person after a decade of begging; or the barroom novelist with pages 1 and 2 of his notebook filled and the rest forever empty. But there is also a generous portion of Peter Pan in every person who does not immediately take up job, marriage, and family in his or her early adult years, and this group includes large numbers of artists and would-be artists.

After perfectionism and narcissism (and feeding into both), the *puer aeternus* phenomenon is thus one of the great cornerstones of writer's block. By not writing, one is obeying the urgent inner command not to define oneself, not to grow and develop into that sad and limited creature, a minor (or possibly even a never-published) poet or whatever. Instead, one stays interestingly, *potentially* great the rest of one's life. It is a phenomenon that occurs not merely among people who daydream a great deal and write very little but also (as we shall see in Chapter 11) among people who show a tremendous early promise and have a great deal of attention focused on their first works. To leave the limelight of precocity and enter the gray world of slow maturation can become a frightening, impossible step to take. F. Scott Fitzgerald's dictum, "There are no second acts in American lives," applies here. For a *puer*, Act I is the whole show, curtain calls included.

Most commonly, however, eternal youths produce no early significant work while secretly nourishing a sense of their own specialness. The hero of Robert Musil's *Man Without Qualities*, a classic *puer*, "feels himself to be like a stride that could be taken in any direction." To such a person, "concreteness suggests craftsmanship, and getting down to craftsmanship means dirtying one's hands."

To be fair, it is true that every serious artist in his or her early years partakes of some of these qualities. Many evolving writers experience a prolonged and dreamy early development in which work comes with painful slowness. But even though the temptation to slide backward into undemanding fantasy is very strong, these awkward beginners are gradually developing, though with unbelievable slowness; at the end of the century, the cereus blossom will open—but not a minute before.

How are such artists different from the writer-to-be who carries her fragments of stories to the café like talismanic objects every day for years and years? They are hardly different at all, except that, in the case of the writer, *finally* something happens: A corner is turned, paradise is lost, and the eternal child enters the world of age and death. But the breakthrough does not usually occur until other emotional bonds that keep the *puer* or *puella* in cocoonlike suspension are broken as well; for here artistic growth is absolutely linked to personal growth.

Let us take the case of the Brontë sisters and their brother Branwell as an example. Charlotte, Emily, Anne, and Branwell enjoyed the archetypal writer's childhood in their widower father's parsonage, a sheltered, exaggeratedly insular environment in which, for lack of outside visitors or amusement, they invented the land of Angria, an imaginary African kingdom with an elaborate history and a vast array of characters. Led always in their fantasies by Branwell, chief instigator and the most brilliant of the lot, the Brontë children recorded their Angrian chronicles in volume upon volume of minuscule coded script.

When childhood ended, the sisters proceeded in turn to their humble jobs as governesses, while Branwell, the young star, awaited his shining destiny as a famous author. It never came. He took and lost many menial positions, succumbed to alcoholism, and died early with none of his ambitions realized. A prolific and talented writer as a child, he was hopelessly blocked as a man. His sisters, perhaps because they were women and thus more protected from worldly expectations, were able, by dint of slow and painful labor, to convert the images of their childhood Nirvana into adult art, thereby winning their own personal victories against a seductive and claustrophobic past. Branwell was unable to perform this rite of passage. In an unfinished fragment of a novel, he gave his hero this familiar *puer*'s lament: "There are plenty of paths in this life. Which shall I take? Only they all require walking to get on them." After what he called in this same fragment the "summit of childhood," Branwell could not bear to descend (as he saw it) from the world of infinite possibility into the world of limited acts.

Those eternal youths who, unlike Branwell, live on, bear the heavy burden of their aborted emotional development and unrealized talent.

As Samuel Coleridge's own *puer* son Hartley put it:

> *Nor child, nor man,*
> *Nor youth, nor sage, I find my head is grey,*
> *For I have lost the race I never ran:*
> *A rathe December blights my lagging May;*
> *And still I am a child, tho' I be old,*
> *Time is my debtor for my years untold.*

On a more hopeful note, we must also remember that the numbers of ex-*pueri* and *puellae* among practicing writers are legion. This time of fantasy and inactivity often proves to be the extended incubation period that is finally, in one's thirties and forties or even later, superseded by a productive career. Still other artists manage to grow up, after a fashion, within their work, while remaining eternal youths in other areas of their lives; in later years, alcoholism or mental illness may undermine their abilities or cut short their working lives.

COMING DOWN TO EARTH

Typically, *pueri* are not busy people; they have too much, not too little, time in which to write. There is a trust fund, an easy part-time job, or some other source of minimal financial support in the background—the perfect setup for a writer, right? Not necessarily. Often, those who have plenty of free time in which to write are precisely the ones who are least able to exploit this opportunity; the lack of boundaries in their lives causes them to flounder. For the unformed person, limitless time offers just more rope to hang himself with.

Baby's first step, for the eternal youth, often means simply committing oneself to work of any sort, even if it is not writing. The experience of submitting to the rigors of a real job, no matter how menial, can have a beneficial carryover to writing. When free time is suddenly confined to an early hour each day or on the weekend, it gains a value all the unending empty months never had. Especially if you have been able to accomplish next to nothing with all the free time in the world, the constraints imposed by a job may allow you to accomplish far more in those few precious hours that are left. You are entering the world of *limits*, which paradoxically liberates you from the prison of limitlessness. Within this structure, which most of us need very badly in our lives, you can allow yourself an hour a day—before work, during lunch hour, on the weekends—to "play."

Suppose, however, you are experiencing the chief *puer* symptom—chronic daydreaming about writing or being a writer, but very little writing—without partaking of the rest of the syndrome. Suppose you live the "provisional" life only vis-à-vis writing and nothing else. What is the day-to-day manifestation of this block likely to be?

First, if you are experiencing many fantasies about writing without producing anything, you are also likely to be afflicted with the psychological sets described in Chapters 4 and 6—namely, the master-slave vicious circle coupled with inflated expectations. Thus, after a period of immersion in fantasies about writing (and, naturally, yourself as world-famous writer), you are likely to suffer a severe attack of guilt when the plain reality of no writing produced asserts itself. You lash yourself as a lazy, worthless creature and resolve on the spot to get up at dawn and write three, five, eight hours a day for the rest of your natural life.

Even if you get as far as rising at dawn, however, you will certainly not be able to carry out the rest of this drastic regimen; the block immediately rises at this futile attempt at self-tyranny. Instead of understanding it as a signal to ease up and modify your self-demands to something more suitable to your real-life personal habits, however, you mistake this healthy and practical reaction for more laziness. After a long and fruitless struggle against the block (the only real sign of your creativity), you slide slowly back into the comfortable, seductive ooze of your daydreams.

This is a cycle that can easily go on for years, if not a lifetime. How to break it? First of all, if it is a habit of some duration in your life, you must face the difficult fact that it will not transform itself overnight. The transition from *puer* dreams into adult actualization is a developmental process that occurs gradually, much like physical growth, over a period of years. Neither process can be speeded up artificially. If you attempt to pole-vault over your natural rate of development with imaginings of not-yet-achieved grandeur, you can expect the process to take that much longer. And since fantasy is the root of creativity, it is not a habit to be "broken" but one to be gone more deeply into, to be retailored to the demands of one's work. Fantasy is the raw material of art as well as daydreams. Producing a work of art, however, means getting your hands dirty.

Getting to the childlike joy of creative expression, then, sometimes requires traveling in the opposite direction—to maturation, as a person and as an artist. Experiencing completion by working or assuming other mundane responsibilities can bring you either to writing (if that is really what your deepest self proves to want) or to some other activity that finally involves you in life.

When you first take up your burden of limits, it will often seem that you are not going anywhere. In fact, the developmental process is proceeding at a steady rate. Your only requirement is to keep writing—no matter if it seems to you that you are the slowest writer in the world, even if your rate is only a story a year. If you can write and finish just one thing, you have taken a step away from your ghostly dreamland into self-actualization. And each piece you write, no matter how pitiful it seems compared to the great opus you can *imagine* (and possibly even write the first paragraph of), takes you that many more steps along in your gradual conversion from dreamer into writer. A *puer*, after all, is an enchanted creature, half in the other world and half in this; to reverse your bewitchment, you must perform some spells of your own. And writing is exactly that: a hex against oblivion.

If you can endure the seven years of enchantment without giving up, you stand an excellent chance of becoming a real human being—less glamorous than a swan but far more powerful. This metamorphosis will only happen if you first submit yourself to two humiliations: first, *beginning* your writing, and second, since finishing anything is impossible for the true eternal youth, *carrying it through*. Out of that long and tiresome struggle comes grace.

ACTUALIZING THE POSSIBLE

Choose any one of the dozens of story, play, or poem fragments in your personal collection and explore the possibility of finishing it. Be careful not to force an ending or simply stop. Put your heart into a genuine finish and allow yourself the experience of closure, a very important rite of passage for a *puer*. Once completed, your work loses the *potential* of greatness and gains the *actuality* of being what it is, and nothing else.

If you can finish one, try finishing others. Remember that if you suffer from this type of block, it is more valuable (because it is harder) to finish one work than to begin a dozen others. You may discover that the act of completing your work is habit-forming. It is also the best spell-breaker of all.

THE WHOLE IS LARGER THAN THE SUM OF ITS PARTS: Notes and Plans That Refuse to Make a Book

"And all your notes," said Dorothea . . . "All those rows of volumes—will you not make up your mind what part of them you will use, and begin to write the book which will make your vast knowledge useful to the world?"

—George Eliot, *Middlemarch*

For many writers the act of note taking—or even that digni-fied activity "research"—is more than just a prelude to the main event. Mysteriously, it comes to supersede the act of writing and becomes the hurdle they never get past.

Rightly or wrongly, we tend to view the chronic note taker as a certain kind of personality—a less than attractive kind. Eliot's Mr. Casaubon, addressed by his wife in the opening quotation, represents the archetypal note taker—fussy, rigid, and anal retentive. A real-life example is the ethnologist John Peabody Harrington (immortalized in his ex-wife Carobeth Laird's memoirs, *Encounter with an Angry God*), who filled warehouse after warehouse at the Smithsonian with literally tons of dusty notes on American Indian languages but was rarely able, for unexplained rea-sons, to "write them up."

A less extreme form of the note-taking disease, howev-er, flourishes in almost everyone who has had a close en-counter with writing. As a case in point, may we take the vo-luminous historical research you once conducted for your blockbuster novel on Oskaloosa during the Civil War or your notebook full of poignant jottings about a sensitive boyhood/girlhood spent in same? And let us not forget the famous shoebox full of index cards, common accessory of "thesis block" (discussed in Chapter 7), the hapless graduate stu-dent is cursed to cart around until he fulfills the terms of his enchantment. What miracle (or what desperate pact with the Devil) will transform these smeared, thumbed, coffee-stained ink scratches into a single coherent work made up of complete sentences marching proudly one after the other from beginning straight through to a triumphant conclusion?

The only magic that can bring about this transformation

is the act of composition itself, a process so totally removed from note taking that the two might not even be considered part of the same experience. This is the real point: *Note taking is not the same process as writing*. Taking notes is mechanical/analytical, not creative, even when the notes do not detail "hard data" but the soarings of your imagination. Because of the qualitative difference between the two processes, it's harder to make the switch than you might think. Many times it's easier to jump straight from writing one piece to writing another than it is to go from the story's own notes to its composition. The tortured graduate student, in fact, might be better off warming up by writing a short essay on another topic than by indulging in yet another Talmud-like perusal of her notes.

Old notes, like old hamburger, congeal. Over time, notes lose their tenuous connection to the dynamic creation of a work and settle into their own rigid reality. You in turn are no longer connected to the inner wellspring that inspired the notes and begin to relate directly to the notes themselves, now strangely lifeless.

The Irish writer Frank O'Connor made it a point never to record more than four lines of notes before beginning a story because

> if you make the subject of a story twelve or fourteen lines, that's a treatment. You've already committed yourself to the sort of character, the sort of surroundings, and the moment you've committed yourself, the story is already written. It has ceased to be fluid, you can't design it any longer, you can't model it.

Why, then, do we experience the desire to cling to our notes instead of simply doing the writing? Because they possess one unassailable advantage: They are *there*, on paper, in black and white. If you fear that lonely first encounter with a blank page, the temptation to hang on to what you've already managed to capture in the net of your awareness—your notes—is irresistible. They become your security blanket, your protection against the horrors of the Unknown, which you must face during actual composition.

Chronic note taking that never develops into finished work is not necessarily the same as the aversion to completion that characterizes the *puer*, the "eternal child." Rather, it is habitual among people who are obsessive and controlling, who are in fact deathly afraid of losing that control, of opening themselves up to the experience of discovering the unexpected inside themselves. As the psychiatrist Rollo May has observed:

> What people . . . do out of fear of irrational elements in themselves as well as in other people is *to put tools and mechanics between themselves and the unconscious world.* This protects them from being grasped by the frightening and threatening aspects of the irrational experience.

The anxiety that even the prospect of such an encounter generates is enough to send such a person scurrying back to the notebook for yet a further round of fragmented, unconnected (but *controllable*) bits of shorthand about what he is planning, someday, to write.

Obviously, there is note taking and note taking. The foregoing examples represent the extreme end of the spectrum and not the middle, where a nice set of notes is just the kind of reassuring anchor on earth one needs to launch a new work successfully. You do not need to reproach yourself for such a habit; it is necessary and useful. Here we are concerned rather with the obsessive note taking that, by its very difference from the creative process, tends to possess the writer and become an end in itself. The challenge to the chronic note taker is to overcome his fears. Can he be persuaded to let go the edge of the swimming pool and kick off unsupported into deep water?

Let's look at the preliminary stages leading up to the act of composition:

1. The germ of an idea surfaces in your consciousness and you are irresistibly attracted to it.
2. An indeterminate period of gestation takes place in which various details and elaborations suggest themselves that you may or may not be noting down.
3. You begin to write.

The chronic note taker is likely to bog down in stage 2, unwittingly locking his potential butterfly inside a stone cocoon. This cocoon often takes the form of a prospectus or grant proposal. Hundreds of thousands more prospectuses have been written in this world than actual books. Once committed to paper, an outline can kill a half-born work by systematizing it too early. There's nothing left to imagine; the joy of discovery is gone.

Sometimes the block that prevents you from making the transition from notes to writing is there because the project you have contemplated is simply too overwhelming and ambitious for your present level of ability. This is what happened to Coleridge, who was forever accepting advances from publishers for outlines of twelve-volume metaphysical or geographical works that never quite materialized. The more grandiose the plan, the cleverer the table of contents, the more immense the block.

Organization and planning are helpful and necessary, especially in beginning a long work such as a novel, but how easily these means become ends in themselves! After staring at the empty page in the typewriter, you turn back to the busy work of fussing with those potsherds, your notes, with pleasure and relief. Taking notes becomes the perfect sanctuary in which to hide so that you can avoid facing the fact that your ego is overdetermining what you are planning to write. An outline or set of notes that paralyzes you instead of inspiring you can be read as your conscious attempt to assume total control of the situation instead of allowing yourself to be guided by your creative energies.

Suppose you have written an outline for a novel that calls for a certain amount of factual or historical research. You go to the library, read extensively, take copious notes. It's fun, it's structured, and it's safe. But it is *not synonymous with the creative act*. Unfortunately, the security of note taking is so addicting that the more you do, the harder it gets to go back to the scary part—writing. One way to avoid this impasse is not to give up the regular creative experience while you are in the midst of note taking. Allot a portion of your time every day to writing something else, and the transition from planning to actual creating in your major project will be effortless.

Or suppose you interrupted a writing career to work or raise children. For years you have carried the idea for a long project, but all you have been able to do is make notes on it. When the time finally arrives to begin, you may find it virtually impossible to write because you have been training all along for a totally different activity—note taking. In effect, you were training all those years for the Boston Marathon by describing the act of running instead of doing a little running every day. A better way to keep your hand in, if you are planning for the future, is to spend the same amount of time on *actual composition*—of whatever you please, however short or nonsensical—that you spend on note taking and dreaming. (Once you are accustomed to it, this can be just as much fun as reading or taking notes.) In this way you *stay* a writer, just as the person who continues running stays a runner, thereby preparing yourself far better for your long project than the person with ten volumes of notes and no immediate creative experience in her fingertips.

DEADLINES

Proposals, promises of books to be, are often associated with deadlines. Writers respond in wildly differing ways to this type of constraint, namely, an outer-world demand placed on their inner-world activities. One of literary history's severest deadlines was successfully met by Dostoevski, who in a scant four months was forced to write an entire novel of approximately five hundred pages (*The Gambler*) while completing an equally long one (*Crime and Punishment*) or forfeit the rights to all his previous works to an unscrupulous publisher. (He dictated them, one in the morning and one in the afternoon, to a stenographer who became his second wife.)

Some writers cannot produce at all unless a deadline looms on the horizon. Others freeze at the slightest hint of outside pressure. Since we learn very early which of these two camps we belong to, it makes sense to try, as much as possible, to order our creative environment according to what we know about our own limitations. If you are a deadline-dreader and must actually produce a work by a given date, you must try to start on it early enough to maintain the illusion of working under no deadline at all—or, if the deadline is extremely tight, give serious thought to the advisability of committing yourself to it at all. You must respect your unconscious rhythms enough to give them all the space they need to operate in. Forcing your creative child to produce within a time frame it cannot manage will result in a block.

Conversely, if you are incapable of writing *anything* without a time limit, it makes sense to manufacture deadlines where they don't already exist. This can be done by announcing a finish date to other interested parties such as your agent or publisher or by deciding to make your work an entry in a competition. Once the deadline has been externalized in this fashion, you are free to believe it is a binding commitment.

ANNOUNCING YOUR INTENTIONS

There is in the air about a man a kind of congealed
jealousy. Only let him say he will do something and
that whole mechanism goes to work to stop him.
                                        —*John Steinbeck*

Telling the world about a deadline is one thing; telling it everything else can produce a lethal block. Announcing your literary plans is an activity closely related to note taking, though it usually involves the spoken rather than the written word. Like note taking, it is intended to calm your inner anxiety—or panic—about jumping off the cliff. Nevertheless, it often serves only to distance you further from undertaking your work. The poet John Berryman's wife makes this testimony about a long poem Berryman planned to write:

> He talked about it so much I suspected he was willing it into being, for I had learned that the chances of a project coming to fruition were in inverse proportion to the amount he discussed it. This was especially true if the talk was high-keyed, and, to my ears, forced, which meant to me that it was make-work, busy-work, anxiety-relieving work—always plausible, always interesting to hear about; not, however, the real thing.

Of this habit (and what writer has not indulged in it at some point?), the novelist Anne Tyler, who "cannot bear to hear people talk about their writing," said: "If they're talking about a plot idea, I feel the idea is probably going to evaporate. I want to almost physically reach over and cover their mouths and say, 'You'll lose it if you're not careful.' "
Some writers, of course, can spill the beans before, during, and after writing their project, with no noticeable adverse effects. Once again, it is up to you to determine your

own specific limits and preferences: At what exact moment does the outline become the Outline or does describing the project to others replace the "real thing"? That there is such a point for every writer is indisputable.

BREAKING OUT OF JAIL

I chart a little first—lists of names, rough synopses of chapters, and so on. But one daren't overplan; so many things are generated by the sheer act of writing.
—Anthony Burgess

Whether you are announcing your intention to the world at large or only to yourself via your notes, you must be sensitive to the moment when you cross the line from true preparation to—let's be honest—stalling. Now, it may be that your unconscious had a valid reason for stalling; some unresolved emotional or technical impasse connected with the piece you have conceived makes you not quite ready to carry it to full term. In such a case, you must be flexible enough to heed the block and set your notes aside *before* you overwork them. This way they will be fresh when the time comes to sit down and do the real creative work.

But what if you have passed this point already? What if you have accidentally gone too far with your notes so that they now imprison you? How can you break out of jail?

Step 1 is to *dis*organize yourself, immediately. Put away your notes. Or if you can't quite bring yourself to let go that much, mess them up. Spread a little chaos into your work; it can produce wonderful results. You may have nailed down too much; now you must let some of it go. Simplify and unstructure your notes. Get rid of those Roman numerals. Use images or actual sentences from the projected piece as your anchor points instead of analytical comments *about* the characters, action, scenery, etc. Best of all, *write the first sentence.*

You will discover, once you begin actually writing the piece, how much closer you have moved to the mysterious unknown center of your story-to-be by imagining it instead of describing it. Moreover, you now have something down on paper that requires no translation from the analytical mode to the imaginative mode; you have actually taken the first steps down the road of discovery that constitutes the creative process.

Many writers need no more incentive to start than this. Others prefer to work out the action in some detail before beginning. Either way, however, it is still impossible to anticipate everything, least of all the texture and final impact of the work. If you are a prisoner of your notes, you may find that it is far safer *not* to capture every last detail before you begin to write; otherwise, you cheat yourself of the pleasure of spontaneous discovery. Start dismantling the rational superstructure now. When your orderly, lifeless notes are in sufficient shambles, the potential work of art they have suffocated will come alive again. Then you'll be ready to start the real adventure.

LETTING GO THE EDGE OF THE SWIMMING POOL

You face a congealed project. Try the following steps:

1. Write something entirely different off the top of your head, without notes of any kind.

2. Reapproach the blocked project—cautiously. Either put the notes completely away or destructure them as indicated in this chapter.

3. Write.

4. If nothing happens, shelve this project for the time being; it may still be too radioactive. Reenter the world of the living and go on to something else.

CHAPTER 9

BEATING A LIVE HORSE: Writing Over the Block, Obsessive Rewriting

Perhaps in order to write a really great book, you must be rather unaware of the fact. You can slave away at it and change every adjective to some other adjective, but perhaps you can write better if you leave the mistakes.

—Jorge Luis Borges

In most cases, once you have passed the note-taking stage, the next logical step is to begin writing. As we saw in the last chapter, this is often the crucial point where your nerve fails and you hesitate, fearing the act of creation. If you make the decision to go ahead, two further choices await you: (1) You can *force* yourself to write, like the person who becomes a parachutist to overcome a fear of heights (psychoanalysts call this type of compensatory activity "reaction formation"), or (2) you can sit down and allow yourself to write as your imagination leads you.

There is a world of difference between the written products of these two states of mind. The first, as a rule, produces worthless material. The second represents true creation. Norman Mailer describes the difference thus:

> Writing at such a time [against one's inclinations] is like making love at such a time. It is hopeless, it desecrates one's future, but one does it anyway because at least it is an act. Such writing is almost unsprung. It is reminiscent of the wallflower who says, "To hell with inhibitions, I'm going to dance." The premise is that what comes out is valid because it is the record of a mood. . . . If you can purge it, if you get sleep and tear it up in the morning, it can do no more harm than any other bad debauch.

By forcing the block, overriding it, you may be prematurely tearing the curtains away from a delicate half-formed something not ready for the full light of consciousness. How often have you heard someone—or yourself—announce: "Tomorrow I'm going to sit down and *try* to write"? The very way this sentiment is expressed signals that an inner conflict regarding writing versus not writing is going on and that the person has decided to "take himself in hand" by forcing the issue. Self-commands of this sort, as we have seen, are always risky. A more cautious, less conflicted way of sneaking up on the problem would be to say, "Tomorrow I'm going to sit down and see what happens. If I write, fine. If I don't write, fine." Allowing yourself the blameless option not to write is very difficult for most writers. But consider that the blame itself may be causing the not writing.

When you sit down in the spirit of *trying* to write (as opposed to allowing yourself to write) and actually manage to come up with something, how do you feel afterward? Excited and pleased? Or merely grimly satisfied that the dreaded chore has been accomplished, one way or another? If you feel the second way, the quality of your writing may very well mirror your inner resentments and ambivalence about being forced to do it.

But, you say, isn't this what creative discipline is all about? Isn't the ability to sit down in front of the typewriter every day, regardless of mood, the mark of the true professional? Isn't it a beginner's fallacy to believe that one must wait to be "inspired"? Haven't we all been taught, after all, that genius is nine-tenths perspiration and one-tenth inspiration? How am I going to perspire if I don't get busy and start to work? etc., etc.

The answers are not simple. Yes, most "professionals" do sit down in front of the typewriter every morning, but this is not true of very many beginners (less than ten years of serious writing), intermediates (ten to fifteen years), or even those advanced writers who may follow a more tortuous and conflicted, but no less valid, path to composition—"the 'beginning late and long choosing' of genius, the crabwise approach to perfection," as Cyril Connolly (a self-confessed blocked writer) has put it. Few are prolific right from the start (except for those logorrheists I will examine in Chapter

11). If you are blocked, the reasons for your resistance must be satisfactorily resolved before you can plunge ahead and start perspiring; you cannot leapfrog over any step in your creative development. This natural brake is a great blessing because it compels your ego to follow the timing of your unconscious. The block represents the taming of an overeager will that must learn painfully and slowly how to adapt itself to the deeper rhythms of the psyche.

The key, of course, is to measure yourself against yourself, not against others. Whether you are in the first years of your writing career or any other stage, there is no reason why you should torture yourself with comparisons to other writers and their output. Your whole attention, in fact, should be focused not on what you *ought* to be doing, but on those unforced patterns of composition that seem to be emerging of their own accord from your unconscious. If you can make this kind of early surrender to yourself and to your deepest creative needs for expression, the chances of your being blocked greatly diminish. Equally, your chances of enjoying a steady, uninterrupted flow of composition ten years down the road greatly increase.

Surrender, not control, as Delacroix said, is always the path. It is only when that hidden, inaccessible side of you says "yes" that you can safely proceed with writing. When your will senses an impenetrable block rising and you have gently tested a number of ways around it, none of which has worked, you must accept a temporary truce and knock at the door of another project—and keep knocking at doors all over the neighborhood until someone lets you in. If instead you stubbornly remain at the locked door in front of you to huff and puff and blow it down, you will enter an empty house—your creative child will have fled in dismay.

If you have been writing for a number of years and your block is chronic, you must be prepared to accept your condition totally, as opposed to railing against it or forcing it. You must, in short, give up your dreams of that instant miraculous transformation always just around the corner and surrender to the block. For once, be deliberate and direct—be conscious—in your decision not to write, instead of letting your unconscious do the work for you. "Take responsibility" (as an overworked phrase has it) for not writing. Quit forcing and stop writing. Give the block a chance to speak to you. This act of surrender, if performed wholeheartedly, should cause you to experience tremendous relief.

OBSESSIVE REWRITING

A first novel is like a first pancake; you have to throw it out.

—Anon.

Forced writing often leads into another kind of nonwriting— namely, the compulsion to rework projects to death. As a delaying tactic that keeps you from new writing, obsessive rewriting is a highly effective manifestation of writer's block. Like note taking, it is something to be let go of so that you can get on with the real work.

Letting go of rewriting must be distinguished from the habit of junking a promising work, like the schoolboy who torched his airplane drawing, because you lack the patience and/or skills to bring your project to full term. Here I refer to the tendency to kill a living work by repeated surgery, amputations, transplants, skin grafts, and the like under the merciless glare of your analytical (not creative) attention. After many tries, you, the mad scientist, produce a patchwork monster that bears little resemblance to your original conception. And, half-consciously recognizing that you have created a golem, you must struggle with the compulsive temptation to continue the revision in a vain attempt to recapture what has been lost. But it is too late. The work, like pastry crust, has been overhandled. Say a few prayers over it and move on.

Some writers, especially beginners, stumble here. They cannot let go, cannot accept that reworking will never change a sow's ear into a silk purse. They are determined to *will* the defunct project back to life by means of even more extreme measures: For example, how about telling it in the present tense rather than the past? Pick out a minor character in the story and retell the whole thing through that person's eyes? And so another year or two passes in which the quality of the writing experience comes to resemble not a master jeweler polishing a diamond, but a cat torture-killing a mouse.

An archetypal story: A young man lives in the country writing stories and novels while supporting himself as a carpenter and odd-job man (for urbanites, substitute taxi driver). It is a lonely, difficult life with no worldly rewards, not even the basic validation of seeing his works in print. He is a talented writer, but many other equally talented writers are competing with him for the pitifully few outlets of publication. Moreover, his works, while competent, lack a certain something—spirit, technique?—to carry them the full distance into art. Aware that this something always eludes him, he relentlessly pursues it via the holy rite of revision. In fact, composition for our carpenter/author has come to play more and more a subsidiary role as he concentrates on endlessly toying with each word he has ever written. He carries a tattered copy of his novel by his side wherever he goes, proof to the world that he really is a writer, not a carpenter—but also in case the quintessential revision should suddenly strike him. What really eludes him, though, is the freshness of effort brought about by a constant assault on the new and unknown. By clinging to the relics of his writing past, he is traveling in the opposite direction from artistic growth.

Of course, many writers work in an antlike fashion, creeping ahead only with the greatest reluctance. This habit of holding on to the past maddens its sufferers. Why, *why* can't they simply dash off one story or chapter after another, the way so-and-so does? For some, this glacierlike pace turns out to be a natural rate of development, which no power on earth can speed up or alter in any way. It is, however, still development. Obsessive rewriting that goes beyond these limits is *arrested* development, and to be avoided.

At some point during their revision of a work, most writers experience a distinct feeling of closure. The obsessive reviser *never* experiences closure. The piece exists in a permanent unhealthy symbiosis with its author. Psychologically, this lack of closure functions in the same way as not writing anything at all, or writing only in fragments—for you can never be judged for what you have not completed. This impasse represents an incubation period that goes on too long. As we saw in Chapter 7, the creative womb exerts a powerful attraction on all sorts of writers to keep postponing their entry into the world of completed (therefore finite and limited) works—whether they are an "eternal child" who imagines everything and writes nothing, a note taker who writes an outline instead of a book, or an obsessive rewriter who, like many house remodelers, refuses to acknowledge that the end must come.

If you find yourself still tied to a work you could have just as easily set aside years ago, your underlying reasons may bear examination. Sometimes your motivation may be only fear of moving on into the unknown—but there may be other compelling factors. For example, consider a first novel about a first marriage, where an emotional tie above and beyond technical or artistic problems keeps you joined to your work. (Gore Vidal has remarked that American novels are "autobiographies, usually composed to pay off grudges.")

Now, an extreme reaction to such an insight into your

own work is typically to say: "Right! Not only this book but this whole episode in my life was sick, sick, sick!" and toss the manuscript into a blazing fire. For some, such a drastic separation might bring relief, but my own instinct is that this is more master-slave behavior. By destroying the manuscript you are *forcing* closure—and how! Afterward, in calmer moments, you are likely to experience strong grief and regret at the violence you have inflicted on yourself. What is wrong with simply putting the manuscript aside? If you can manage to leave it alone, the passage of time may provide the closure you are unable to give it. Reading it years later, you will have a much sharper perspective on its merits and demerits. Once you destroy it, however, you will have lost forever any opportunity for perspective.

But finally, we should never forget that assiduous rewriting, as part of the drive for perfection, is a godlike curse because it is also the means to full consummation of the artist's vision. The vice of obsessive rewriting can be turned to your advantage as a stylist. When asked how often he rewrote a piece, the humorist S.J. Perelman replied that he averaged about thirty-seven times:

> I once tried doing thirty-three, but something was lacking, a certain—how shall I say—*je ne sais quoi*. On another occasion, I tried forty-two versions, but the final effect was too lapidary. . . .

And there is the story of the guard in a French museum who intervened in horror as an elderly white-bearded gentleman whipped out a paintbrush and began to deface a priceless Vuillard. It was the artist himself (with his friend Monet as watchdog) indulging in a final revision.

BEATING A LIVE HORSE

Select a project you have been endlessly picking at and getting nowhere with. *Put it away.* Allow yourself the fun and freedom of starting a new work—nothing as important as the picked-over masterpiece, of course. Tell yourself you're just killing time while saving up energy for that one last rewrite. Tell yourself you *ought* to be hacking away on the rewrite right now (this is a good way to guarantee you don't do it), but for once you are going to indulge yourself by fooling around with something new.

The results may surprise you.

CHAPTER 10

HAVE YOU A GLASS SLIPPER IN A SIZE 13?
Forcing Your Talent into the Wrong Mold

I started writing poetry when I was six and stopped when I was twenty-six because it was getting a little better, but not terribly much. When I was fifteen I wrote seven hundred pages of an incredibly bad novel. . . . Then, when I was nineteen I wrote a couple hundred pages of another novel, which wasn't very good either. I was still determined to be a writer. And since I was a writer, and here I was twenty-nine years old and I wasn't a very good poet and I wasn't a very good novelist, I thought I would try writing a play, which seems to have worked out a little better.

—Edward Albee

Among the several ways of forcing creative energy into a sterile corner is the imposition of a whole false writing persona, whether style or genre, upon yourself. The way out of this impasse involves the difficult task of discovering your true identity as a writer—a lifelong, constantly evolving process with no guideposts except blind instinct to tell you whether you are on the right track. In this context, writer's block serves as a lie-detector test that determines whether you are forcing yourself down a particular path for reasons of ego and/or finances and/or others' advice or example, or are writing straight from the heart. Moreover, even writing straight from the heart can cause problems if your conscious self and your unconscious self have diametrically opposed notions about what direction your writing should take. In time, their disagreement will make itself known in the form of a substantial block.

This is another version of the battle of "ought" versus "want" discussed in Chapter 4. In the classic "ought" bind, you have constructed a long list of how your career "ought" to go and what sorts of things you "ought" to be writing, to the point where your self-demands have effectively estranged you from your true sources of inspiration. Whole writing careers have been tragically sacrificed on the altar of "ought." It is a special brand of suicide that can be performed by writing beneath, above, or even alongside the true current of your creativity: The esoteric writer attempts a "breakthrough" book to reach a mass audience; the author of Westerns tries to "get serious."

A good example would be the short-story writer or poet who is urged (or urges himself) to write a big fat novel for purposes of wider readership. Many poets and short-story writers have made the transition successfully, and for reasons no more noble than that just stated. Furthermore, it is always good to stretch and test your abilities by trying a new medium. But if you are one of those special few who are only made to write poems or short stories, a big fat novel in outline or note form is all that is likely to result. The short-story writer Katherine Anne Porter, prodded by her editor to write a novel, labored twenty years to produce *Ship of Fools*; it was a form she ultimately admitted she did not feel comfortable with.

Or suppose you are an unrecognized writer (unpublished or published) with serious aspirations. You decide to "go for it" and attract the world's attention by writing (1) a murder mystery, (2) a historical romance, or (3) soft pornography for a "quick sale." Now, a variety of strange things may happen when you decide to take what seems to be an eminently practical, worldly-wise step: You may find to your surprise that you have a natural facility in one of these areas—in fact, a greater facility than for your earlier "serious" experimental efforts, and, having let go the false snobbery that kept you chained to inappropriate forms, you will have discovered your true mode of expression.

On the other hand, you may find yourself hopelessly blocked. You make the interesting discovery that it is just as hard to write popular fiction as it is to write anything else. Popular fiction is constructed from an intricate set of rules that may seem technically quite difficult—far more difficult, in terms of such factors as plot development, than what you may be used to writing. Nine times out of ten, your thriller or romance will lie half finished on your desk, casualty not only of the nuts-and-bolts facility it takes to write one of these books but of your own inner conflicts as well: Your creative child may still prefer to be writing prose poems. If you continue to force yourself down this path, you may ultimately prove successful and thus trigger still another conflict, this time a lifelong one. You are, after all, what you write, and in one of those mysterious flip-flops of fate, you risk becoming the popular writer who "should have" stayed serious.

Many writers commit this great mistake: They assume that writing commercial fiction is easier than writing "literature." Both in technique and in spirit, it is not. It is simply the mode some writers can express themselves in and others cannot. For someone not meant to write it at all, the results can be grotesque. Moreover, and most important, the works of the top "popular" writers, though often naive and badly constructed, possess an indefinable aura of sincerity that their readers unconsciously respond to. These writers *believe* in what they're writing. In their work, they have found the perfect vehicle for their deepest convictions about life (including, incidentally, the right to earn a good living). If you cynically take up a popular genre while your true inclination lies in another direction, you may never do it as effectively as the "naturals" do. You may grow to do it competently, but paradoxically you may never "shine" in the popular eye the way a much less skilled writer does—unless you come to believe in it, too. Conversely, if popular fiction draws you more powerfully than any other type of literature, you are wrong to feel you must strive to write any "higher" than you naturally do. These labels of "highbrow" and "escapist" are virtually meaningless anyway.

Another example: Suppose you have enrolled in a creative writing class. You submit your first story, a diffuse, ornately written mystical narrative. The instructor, a neorealist in the grand tradition of American truck-stop regionalism, pounces like a tiger, eagerly followed by the rest of the class. You are informed, gently or ruthlessly, that true art consists of clean, spare, seamless prose and not your kind, which he finds imitative, old-fashioned, and unbearably phony. Following the example of several microgenerations of well-intentioned creative writing teachers, he advises you to write about "what you know best"—that is, your immediate external environment—just like the other students, who are dutifully cranking out chronicles of their lives and loves; or, since most of them, including the teacher, are sheltered souls themselves, they often confuse "real life" with low life and produce stories of hitchhikers and hookers that are actually far more romantic, in their way, than anything in *The Thousand and One Nights*.

Now, there is an 80 percent probability that your instructor is dead-on right about your present mode of writing—it *is* awful— and that you have received what you came to the class to get, namely, good advice. But in the other 20 percent of the cases, he will be wrong and you will be right, because those ponderous sentences, as full of seams as a *fin de siècle* fancy dress, are actually your voice, or at least the beginnings of your voice.

How do you know who is really right in this situation? By a simple test: If you have only been imitating, you will find the transition to a different style (though not necessarily the instructor's favored kind) not only relatively easy but also a relief. The change will excite you and expand your sense of artistic possibilities. If, however, you have been truly writing out of the core of your as-yet unformed artistic abilities, you will find any alteration grating and unnatural. Like a lefty being forced to write right-handed, you will constantly backslide into your old ways and your public efforts to please your audience (here, instructor and class) will become even more artificial in a different way, than your initial work. Here, writer's block is an eloquent expression of that side of you that stubbornly refuses to write out of character, no matter how much outside pressure is brought to bear.

Criticism, as discussed in Chapter 5, can exert a tremendous influence on the direction your writing takes. It can also engender the most horrific writing blocks as you attempt to assimilate it. In the desire to improve and perfect your craft, you will find it almost impossible to resist the guidance offered by others, yet the effect of even laudatory remarks is often to throw you off center and out of touch with your own instincts. And if a barrage of negative comments has greeted your latest effort, do you flatly decide it is totally undeserved (arrogant approach) or totally deserved (craven approach)? The truth probably lies somewhere in between, but it is difficult to tolerate the uncertainties. How much easier to declare yourself all the way on one side or the other, thereby closing out crippling doubt!

If you shut out criticism entirely, however, you are losing a chance to grow and to understand more deeply (though probably never fully) the impression your works make on others. On the other hand, if you are so overly impressionable that you accept every comment about your work as Gospel, you are heading for worse trouble. Humbly you promise: "I will *not* write that bad way anymore that nobody likes! I will write the way that has been recommended to me by my betters and be a good boy/girl." A vow like this, however, is doomed to trigger a rebellion in your psyche. Either you experience a severe block or, writing according to others' expectations, you depart from your own need to experiment and your writing develops a glossy, insincere veneer. This development can occur in all sorts of ways that seem relatively benign at first.

To stand the middle ground between these two extremes is the most difficult task of all—to be able to entertain the contradictory possibilities that your writing may be terrible or great or somewhere in between. But this open-minded position is most likely to keep your conscious and unconscious selves in steady dialogue. Whether you possess the strength to do this without losing your balance depends on how carefully you have cultivated that inner instinct the poet Rainer Maria Rilke called conscience:

In artistic work one needs nothing so much as conscience: it is the sole standard. (Criticism is not one, and even the approval or rejection of others active outside of criticism should only very seldom, under unmistakable conditions, acquire influence.) That is why it is very important not to misuse one's conscience in [one's] early years, not to become hard at the place where it lies. It must remain light through everything; one may feel it just as little as any inner organ that is withdrawn from our will. The gentlest pressure emanating from it, however, one must heed, else the scale on which one will later have to test every word of the verses to be written will lose its extreme sensitivity.

If you have not learned how to listen consciously to this internal guide, or if you simply refuse to pay any attention to it, writer's block often intervenes as an unconscious and involuntary ethical self-regulator.

Remember that bending oneself into unnatural poses as a writer is just as likely to occur in the higher realms of literary pursuit as it is in popular or commercial literature. You can prostitute yourself *up* as well as down; many serious writers live as much of a double life as the crassest manipulator of the best-seller racket. Like those readers who proudly display their gold-stamped sets of the great classics but secretly cherish paperback mysteries, such writers often show a tremendous unconscious split between ego and true inclination. Jorge Luis Borges has commented:

> I have known many poets . . . who have written well—very fine stuff—with delicate moods and so on—but if you talk with them, the only thing they tell you is smutty stories or speak of politics in the way that everybody does, so that really their writing turns out to be a kind of sideshow. They had learned writing in the way that a man might learn to play chess or to play bridge. They were not really poets or writers

at all. It was a trick they had learned, and they had learned it
thoroughly.

Why try to be what you think you should be as a writer,
when discovering with humility what you are, no matter how
unpleasant this news may be to your ego (I am a sporadic
writer, I am a writer who will never make a dime, I am a writer who will never be taught in a literature class), carries so
much more inner resonance, both with yourself and with
your readers? I submit that the vast majority of cases of writer's block examined in this book can be labeled healthy, instinctive reactions to an attempt at *self-falsification*—whether you are trying to live up to a self-image as an eight-hour-a-
day writer, a world-famous writer, a perfect writer, a
best-selling writer, your father or mother's idea of a writer, or
whatever. Every writer has within herself a certain setpoint,
a natural and unconscious home base, from which the conscious identity is built. If you have the courage to set aside
the false self-image and simply let the writing be what it
wants to be, the block is very likely to go away.

A tremendous energy is released when you let go, even
temporarily, some of these superficial ambitions and find out
for yourself how you prefer to write. For once, take the opportunity to lose your self-consciousness and do not worry
on one hand if what you are writing is "great" or on the other
if it will "sell." Just as there is no longer a debtor's prison,
there is likewise no writer's prison, either—except the ones
we construct for ourselves. You don't *have* to write any way
at all; *you can write however you please*. Rilke's advice to
the young writer goes equally well for the blocked writer:

> It makes no difference what one writes as a very young per-
> son, just as it makes almost no difference what else one un-
> dertakes. The apparently most useless distractions can be a
> pretext for inwardly collecting oneself. . . . One may do

anything; this alone corresponds to the whole breadth life has. But one must be sure not to take it upon oneself out of opposition, out of spite toward hindering circumstances, or, with others in mind, out of some kind of ambition. . . .

Is such advice too high-flown and impractical for a writer who makes his/her living at the trade, facing the realities of the publishing market? First of all, if it is true that what you may write in such a relaxed frame of mind is unpublishable, it is even more true that what you *don't* write in a blocked state is unpublishable, too. Rilke's statement is the cornerstone of all creative endeavor. As we have seen again and again, writers who are seriously and chronically blocked are usually out of touch not only with the simple, the innocent, and the playful but with their own basic identity. They need to go back to square one and take their first stumbling steps again, suspending all sophisticated judgment and creative directives until they have reestablished genuine contact with their inner sources.

But what if you feel genuinely trapped in your present mode of writing and want to make a break? What if you are experiencing a block in your attempts to leap from the confining but comfortable known to the terrifying unknown? This situation of *authentic* change of writing roles deserves to be examined more closely.

CHANGING YOUR WRITING PERSONA

Some years ago, the journalist Tom Wolfe was faced by a "notes that refuse to make a story" block. As usual, this block masked a deeper creative dilemma. Sent to cover a hot rod and custom car show by the *New York Herald Tribune*, he had dutifully turned in "exactly the kind of story any of the somnambulistic totem newspapers in America would have

come up with." Wolfe knew he had another story underneath, but it was more than just a different story—inside him
a whole new way of looking at the world was struggling to
emerge. The conflict between this surge of creativity and his
commitment to old-fashioned journalese produced a massive
writing block.

Fascinated by the custom cars as a form of new proletar-
ian art, Wolfe followed up the story in California for *Esquire*
magazine but found himself totally unable to write the second story in the usual way. Back in New York, he sat hopelessly over his typewriter and finally called Byron Dobell,
the managing editor of *Esquire*, to confess defeat. Dobell in-
structed Wolfe to type his notes for someone else to write up:

> So about 8 o'clock that night I started typing the notes out in
> the form of a memorandum that began, "Dear Byron." I
> started typing away, starting right with the first time I saw
> any custom cars in California. I just started recording it all,
> and inside of a couple of hours, typing along like a madman, I
> could tell that something was beginning to happen. By mid-
> night this memorandum to Byron was twenty pages long and
> I was still typing like a maniac . . . . I wrapped up the mem-
> orandum about 6:15 A.M., and by this time it was 49 pages
> long. I took it over to *Esquire* as soon as they opened up,
> about 9:30 A.M. About 4 P.M., I got a call from Byron Dobell.
> He told me they were striking out the "Dear Byron" at the
> top of the memorandum and running the rest of it in the maga-
> zine.

The result was "The Kandy-Kolored Tangerine-Flake
Streamlined Baby," a bit of journalistic history. Wolfe's description of this breakthrough into a voice and style uniquely
his own is an eloquent statement of the suffering one endures
when trying to write against the grain of one's nature—and
the indescribable relief experienced when one lets go the in-

hibitions and the "shoulds." That click, that feeling of release, is always the key, regardless of what your ego or the current wisdom may be saying. Wolfe had been locked into the confines of the traditional news story, which had suited neither him nor his subject. Heeding the block meant having the courage to move in another direction, though in Wolfe's case this was a spontaneous and unconscious act born of desperation rather than a deliberately thought-out decision.

Discovering who you are as a writer at any given time in your life can be an experience that causes a major upheaval, even to the point of changing you from a poet to a dramatist (Edward Albee), from a novelist to a poet (Thomas Hardy), or from a fiction writer to a journalist (Truman Capote, Norman Mailer). Human nature being what it is, however, many writers unhappy with who they *really* are nourish daydreams of being quite a different sort of writer. Sir William Gilbert, for example, the librettist of the inspired musical theater team of Gilbert and Sullivan, wanted desperately to be a writer of great stage tragedies, a task for which he was entirely unsuited. Similarly, writers who have spent the bulk of their careers in journalism are always announcing that they are about to take up fiction. In these cases, the dream of change is no true goal but an ego ideal—as well as a sneaky way of putting down one's real accomplishments.

It is thus a delicate matter to determine whether a new medium is meant for your talents or whether changing into it represents only a compensatory daydream. Usually, however, the problem takes care of itself in the sense that what a writer ends up writing the most of is probably what she was "meant" to do—that is, it is what she truly *wants* to do. The only way to find out if your talent belongs in a different genre is to make the leap and try. Even if you fall on your face, you will at least have had the satisfaction of exploring that alternate path; you will never again have to wonder if that was really the road you ought to have taken.

If you are holding yourself back because what you now write is publishable and you fear that what you will try to write is not, consider this: If what you now write makes you either miserable or unable to write at all, do you really have such a low estimate of your potential in another area that you believe that what you *want* to write can never be published? If you put off the experiment too long, if you squelch your desire to explore some of the less conventional byroads of your psyche, your writing muscles may stiffen in one mode and you may lose the creative flexibility to realize your dream.

It is human nature to be lazy, and that is why writer's block is such a useful, benign, and ultimately blessed instrument of our higher selves. Only when an impassable roadblock suddenly rears up on our accustomed route (or rut) do we ever consider trying another path.

FINDING THE SHOE THAT FITS

1. List by genre, category, and style the kind of a writer you think you *ought* to be. (You may be surprised by the half-submerged assumptions and demands you have swallowed about yourself.) Can you state briefly what you are? What you *prefer* to write?

2. If you were to start all over again as a writer, would you pick a different mode of expression? What would it be? Do you have an irresistible desire to try out this mode now, or do you prefer to keep it in the realm of daydream? Have you already made attempts in this direction? In actual practice, which mode gives you most satisfaction?

NO CLOISTERED VIRTUE: Using Your Writing to Hide from Life

For my omniscience paid I toll
In infinite remorse of soul.

—Edna St. Vincent Millay
"Renascence"

The Prodigy's Dilemma

Some writers demonstrate precocious talent. In childhood and adolescence, they produce an abundance of stories, poems, essays, often working in extreme emotional and social isolation. And, unlike the *puer* who fails to mature, the prodigy continues to produce well into early adulthood. Typically, he or she grows into an intense, even eccentric young person who may experience a substantial early success.

But then something happens. The prodigy hits the wall—usually in his or her twenties or early thirties, a time when the lingering ghost of childhood must be sacrificed to a full maturity. This is the moment life presents the industrious, ever-productive prodigy with the emotional bill for his too-mature endeavors, which is usually very high.

The first sign that an emotional crisis is in the works is often a sudden halt in the steady outpouring of written material: The prodigy's creative engine begins to run out of steam. This block can be followed by more drastic consequences. Paradoxically (and perhaps unfairly), the hardworking prodigy runs a much higher risk of experiencing a nervous breakdown than the perennially blocked *puella*, whose drifting ways allow her to elude all the major emotional passages of life.

Almost every case of precocity involved a parent who has actively encouraged premature achievement, a parent whom the prodigy has always striven to please. Not surprisingly, possibly the biggest bumper crop of literary prodigies was produced in the Victorian era, with its intense, even claustrophobic focus on family life. This special brand of domestic religion spawned an alarming number of young ge-

nius acolytes, shadow extensions of dominant, often ambitious parents. The mental sufferings of these prodigies in later life were as spectacular as their early achievements. Charles Lamb, Samuel Taylor Coleridge, the Brontës, John Ruskin, John Stuart Mill, Robert Louis Stevenson, the American Margaret Fuller—all these writers, their identities heavily bound up in the wishes of their parents, suffered mental crises at the crucial transition from adolescence to adulthood. In place of initiation into autonomy, the prodigy substitutes a nervous breakdown.

Typically, the prolific child prodigy who doesn't survive the rite of passage into adulthood remains blocked forever. Others have survived against all odds. The precocious H. P. Lovecraft, reared in isolation by a schizophrenic mother, took to his bed at age seventeen and refused to get up, by all signs headed toward schizophrenia himself. At some point, however, he seems to have mysteriously turned himself around, rising from bed of his own accord to lead a sane, if highly eccentric, life.

Why should the prospects for prodigies, seemingly bright, actually be so dim? We have said that art is playful—and we know that fantasy is an important and positive element of a happy childhood. Art and fantasy, however, are not synonymous; the artist is not himself a "creative child." And although an early immersion in this most monastic and solipsistic of disciplines often serves many sensitive adolescents as a needed sanctuary in which to hide from the emotional and sexual storms of impending adulthood, to enter too early, and to stay too long, is to miss (at great emotional cost) the transition to an adult sensibility.

In the end, such a retreat can turn out to be no sanctuary at all but a new and terrible kind of prison. The writer is stuck with a devouring technique that has already digested the meager life experiences of its very young owner and now begins, as it were, to feed off living tissue. John Ruskin, at age

eleven writing two-thousand-line poetic commentaries on travels with his parents, by age twelve had written a poem plaintively titled, "Want of a Subject." John Stuart Mill complained that the premature cultivation of his intellect had left him "stranded at the commencement of my voyage, with a well-equipped ship and a rudder, but no sail; without any real desire for the ends which I had been so carefully fitted out to work for."

The self-imprisonment of precocious talent is vividly described in a fictional portrait of a teenage poet by the Czech writer Milan Kundera:

> The poet, banished from the safe enclosure of childhood, longs to go out into the world, but because he is afraid of the real world he constructs an artificial, substitute world of verse. He lets his poems orbit around him like planets around the sun. He becomes the center of a small universe in which nothing is alien, in which he feels everything is constructed out of the familiar materials of his own soul. Here he can achieve everything which is so difficult "outside."

Kundera adds, cruelly, that such a young poet's true interaction with the outside world only begins when everyone laughs at the grandiose emotions of his verses, rudely bursting the amniotic bubble of vanity that envelops him.

But if such healing laughter never comes, there is the added penalty of the solitary nature of writing, which can shut an already too sequestered person even further away from the world. Considering all this, a prodigy who suddenly becomes blocked may actually be experiencing a healthy signal from the unconscious—a signal that he is not ready to be locked up inside himself. John Stuart Mill temporarily stopped writing at age twenty and viewed his silence afterward with relief, as witness this passage from "Crisis in My Mental History":

It was of no common importance to me at this period, to be
able to digest and mature my thoughts for my own mind only,
without any immediate call for giving them out in print. Had I
gone on writing, it would have much disturbed the important
transformation in my opinions and character, which took
place during those years.

The emotional demands of a lifetime must be met just as
fully by an artist or thinker as by any other person; the writer's block in such cases effectively prevents escape and
avoidance of life. For the time being, at least, the would-be
writer must go out and live his unlived life instead of, in the
words of the poet Stephen Shrader, "leaving by the closet
door."

In the America of twenty or thirty years ago, "living
life" meant basically one thing: The young writer (always
male) had to hit the road, garnering enough adventures as
hitchhiker, dishwasher, bouncer, and drifter to fill out the bi-
ographical entry on the dust jacket below his picture. But
that conception of life has little to do with the complex emotional adventures every man and woman must weather in a
lifetime, each in his or her uniquely individual way. As Elizabeth Bowen said of Flaubert, it is just as possible to live fully "a life of inner dynamicism which cover[s], geographical-
ly, little space." Life is present everywhere; it is not something "out there," it is "in here" as well. All lives, however,
demand balance and variety between inner and outer
experiences.

Significantly, prodigies who weather the crisis of young
adulthood often abandon fiction and poetry and turn to essay
writing, journalism, and criticism, all of which provide a
strong rational framework that can support a fragile personality at the same time that they conceal emotional underde-
velopment and related conflicts—traits that imaginative
writing mercilessly exposes. Expository writing, an honor-

able profession in its own right, has always been a time-honored detour for the blocked imaginative writer. Victorian England produced the greatest essayists of English literature from its aging prodigies—but not the greatest art.

One reason many prodigies never recover from their creative block in adult life may be unconscious rage against a ruined childhood, sacrificed on the altar of a parent's unfulfilled dreams. Many ex-prodigies live out their adult lives in unconscious dedication to trampling on their parents' "great expectations," even though, for the truly talented, this often means cutting off the nose to spite the face. For this "spite block" finally to be lifted, an elaborate psychological reorientation toward the parents and toward oneself must take place, a therapeutic process that can consume years. Sometimes such conflicts are resolved in the course of a lifetime, sometimes not. Often, the resentment directed against a dominant parent stays unconscious and is expressed in the form of a block; or, if the person is actually able to write, he may be crippled by periodic bouts of self-destructiveness, such as episodes of alcoholism, the function of which is to keep him in a state of childlike dependence, saying to the parent, in effect, "You made me like this—now you can take care of me!"

The prodigy who heeds the block by *living* may never return to writing if (as in many cases) its main purpose was as a sanctuary or a way to please parents and not a true vocation. If you were or are one of those persons, giving up writing is not a failure but affirmation of your true identity on a deep level. Do not allow the great expectations of others—family, friends—who thoughtlessly quiz you ("But what are you doing *now*?") to make you feel guilty once you have made the decision to stop writing. You are not blocked; you have made a decision to do something else with your life. In betraying other people's image of you, you have affirmed your own.

Other ex-prodigies spend years suppressing a real talent

in order to achieve a stronger demand to grow up emotionally, then find their creative impulses reawakening in later life. If you are one of these people who find their resistance suddenly lifted after many years, you can return to writing confident that you are doing it for yourself. Your unconscious has judged you ready to begin again, to distill and shape what you have gained and lost from life.

So if you are a young writer with a substantial *ouevre* behind you and now, in spite of your most earnest desires to continue, face a monumental block, that block is life. Accept it and enter without looking back. If the work is something that truly belongs to you, it will lead you back when you are ready. If it does not, better adventures await you—better because they were meant for you. No man is an island, and it is time to explore the archipelago.

ESCAPING STRONG FEELINGS

You can immerse yourself in the flat white abyss of the page, hide from yourself and your private universe, which will soon explode and vanish.
—*Tadeusz Konwicki*

The temptation to hide out in the putative safety of your imagination when you need to be facing something directly in your emotional life afflicts not only prodigies or ex-prodigies. In the face of tremendous emotional stress, this can happen to any writer at any time. It can arise either because too much unresolved emotion is tied to the project at hand or because an accumulation of avoided problems hangs like a dark cloud over one's entire personal life.

When such an impasse occurs, some find it a relief to turn to expository writing or daily journal keeping, since the delicate and complicated inner equilibrium that imaginative

writing requires is impossible to maintain. At such times a diary can be a real lifesaver, as Kafka attested in his own day-book: "I must hold on here, it is the only place I can." Often, if you simply wait for the storm to pass and the wound to heal, the block lifts of its own accord. But you must constant-ly make a gentle discrimination between justifiable hiberna-tion and outright avoidance of deeper conflicts. Beware that the temporary turning away does not harden into permanent avoidance of either the emotions or the writing. Keep con-stantly checking—keep knocking on the door—to see if you are ready to go back. Only by testing that is constant, gentle, and nonjudgmental will you be able to determine the state of your inner desires.

Another way to trigger the "hideout block" is to seek to construct an artificial womb of peace and tranquility within which to do your writing—the "cabin in the woods" syn-drome discussed in Chapter 2. Some writers do thrive on the cabin in the woods; if that is your accustomed place of com-position, so be it. Others may simply be trying to hide from life itself.

The poet Rilke, plagued by writer's block, was con-stantly fleeing his sculptress wife to find the perfect solitude in which to compose his verses free from the interruption of untidy emotional obligations. To the dispassionate reader—or, more precisely, to the female reader—this kind of state-ment has the distinctly fishy smell of an excuse, not of a noble rationale. And in fact the prisoner of Duino Castle seems to have suffered just as severely from his block away from home as in it.

Art is not a refuge from life; to try to make it that dimin-ishes both the work and its creator. Let the last eloquent word on this subject go to a poet, the late Louise Bogan:

> Poetry is an activity of the spirit; its roots lie deep in the sub-conscious nature, and it withers if that nature is denied, ne-

glected, or negated. . . . A poet emerges from a spiritual crisis strengthened and refreshed only if he has been strong enough to fight it through at all levels, and at the deepest first. One refusal to take up the gage thrown down by his own nature leaves the artist confused and maimed. And it is not one confrontation, but many, which must be dealt with and resolved. The first evasion throws the poet back into a lesser state of development which no show of bravado can conceal. "A change of heart" is the result of slow and difficult inner adjustments. A mere shift in allegiance, if it is not backed up by conflict genuinely resolved, produces in the artist, as it produces in any one, confusion and insincerity. The two great poets of our time, Rilke and Yeats, because they fought their own battles on their own ground, became, first, mature men, and then mature artists. They drew to themselves more and more experience; their work never dried up at the source or bloated into empty orotundity. The later poetry of both is work based on simple expression, deep insight, and deep joy.

LOGORRHEA: AN IMPORTANT NOTE

Let's be brief: The world is overpopulated with words.
—Stanislaw Jerzy Lec

Of all the "hiding from life" blocks, however, none is more striking, and more cleverly disguised as its opposite, than the phenomenon of logorrhea, or compulsive writing. The extraordinarily prolific writer whose phenomenal output flows unchecked is often an object of awe for the blocked writer, who, envying him in the same way that an overweight person envies the anorexic, fails to see that this deluge of words often conceals an inverted case of writer's block. Like Hans Christian Andersen's little dancer who couldn't get the enchanted red shoes off her feet, the compulsive writer liter-

ally cannot stop writing. Compulsive writing is, in fact, a cleverly disguised way of hiding from some of the deeper demands of literary and emotional experience.

How can this be? Simply because for some writers, the act of writing itself has taken on the aspect of a tic or other nervous habit, meaningless except as a temporary relief and flight from anxiety. These writers give birth to book after book, not because their Muse of Realization is on twenty-four-hour-a-day, 365-day-a-year duty, but because they are in flight from their personal demons and writing provides the necessary fortification within which to hide. Malcolm Lowry's biographer, Douglas Day, indulging (perhaps too freely) in a bit of literary psychoanalysis, has speculated that

> ultimately, language—the emission of words—may come to be a defense against the dissolution of the personality. The death-wish, present in us all, is perhaps strongest in the oral type; who, having never really separated himself from the all-encompassing maternal elements, is in gravest danger of subsiding back into it. If he is as acute as Malcolm Lowry was, he may recognize the lethal attraction of silence, and may write copiously, compulsively, in order not to die.

Whether or not denial of a death wish lies at the bottom of compulsive writing, there is no doubt that it constitutes a defense of some sort, armor against unknown terrors, rather than the constant blossoming expression of inner truth. This does not mean that such writers never produce art, but merely that a lot of what they do produce amounts to foot-tapping in between their serious efforts.

To some extent, all humans avoid facing the deeper strata of life. Writing itself is a form of stress that we all try to avoid to the degree we find it stressful. But whereas blocked writers are those who discover their demons directly in the act of writing (and thus instinctively fear writing as an en-

counter with the unknown), compulsive writers experience that confrontation in some other part of their psyches, causing them to flee *into* writing. In either case, the block involves keeping the production of verbiage (which by itself is no more than merely keeping the motor running) distinctly separate from a deeply felt artistic impulse. You cannot really claim you are in the high service of the Muse if you have to write the way other people have to smoke a cigarette.

Since overproduction is a less common form of writer's block than underproduction, it is harder to chart the progress of such writers. Do they occasionally become unable to write? Do they continue their awesome production to their dying day? Or am I merely writing out of the prejudices of modern times, overlooking such eras as the Victorian in England or the Golden Age of Spanish drama, when a voluminous output was standard operating procedure? (Anthony Trollope, dean of Victorian novelists, wrote fifty-four novels in addition to assorted travel books and *belles lettres*; Lope de Vega, Spanish playwright of the sixteenth century, wrote, by his own estimate, fifteen hundred plays.)

In fact, overproducers have been a target of scorn for many modern writers. In answer to the burning question "Which is worse, to write too little or too much?" Cyril Connolly once stated:

> Sloth in writers is always a symptom of an acute inner conflict, especially that laziness which renders them incapable of doing the thing which they are most looking forward to, but their silence is better than . . . overproduction. . . . [S]lothful writers such as Johnson, Coleridge, Greville, in spite of the nodding poppies of conversation, morphia, and horse-racing have more to their credit than Macaulay, Trollope or Scott.

Connolly is saying, in effect, that constipation is a condition

more virtuous than diarrhea. At the least, such an opinion is a useful antidote for (if not an actual product of) the envy and despair a slow writer feels in comparing himself to the logorrheists. And Rilke, while plaintively admitting that

> I lacked that vitality of the great master [Rodin] which, little by little, had put him in a position to meet his inspiration unceasingly with so many work projects that it could not help acquiescing, almost without a pause coming up, to *one* of those offered,

still put his finger on the corresponding literary sin of the "steady" producers when he compared the principled silence of Tolstoi, who had given up his art for a cause, with the vast majority of writers who, with their regular and unremitting output, "were determined by practice and falsification (by 'literature') to conceal the occasional slackening or defection of their fruitfulness." In short, the prolific writer is not necessarily more disciplined than the slow writer; he is likewise obeying the dictates of an instinctive (and uncontrollable) inner rhythm. More, however, is not always better.

THE LINK BETWEEN LIFE AND ART

Think of the most traumatic emotional episode that has happened to you in your recent experience. Describe what effects (good, bad, or none at all) that episode had on your creative work, both while it was going on and afterward. Did you work more intensely during this period? Were you able to work at all?

The time-honored devices of journal and diary keeping, as well as dream recording, allows you to continue writing regularly during such times (as well as providing excellent training during your entire writing career). The daily act of translating reality into language keeps the door wide open for a return to art.

WHOM AM I SPITING?

Can you think of someone in your past or present against whom your writer's block might be directed? Write down the name(s). Why do you want to get even with this person? Is it a satisfying revenge? (Either yes or no is a correct answer.)

BITCH GODDESS/ BASTARD GOD: Success and Writer's Block

Whom the gods would destroy, they first call promising.

—Cyril Connolly

Success is one of those great force fields of life—it attracts, repels, saves, destroys. We are all obliged to come to terms with it according to our uniquely individual situations. Our personal standards of success, however, are inevitably influenced by the stereotypes society presents us. Whether or not we measure up (or down) to these stereotypes constitutes the first identity crisis on the road to defining success in our own terms.

Literary success, even in a multilayered society such as America, is often viewed simplistically as either "commercial," with mass readership and substantial financial reward, or "serious," with far less financial return but critical recognition and kudos. Both these types of success represent fame, of course, the pinnacle of the success pyramid. Because of what Saul Bellow has called America's "major-league atmosphere in literature," most writers, published or unpublished, tend to measure their own success in terms of the handful who have achieved fame. But there are other, no less significant plateaus of success. In a country that seems to contain almost as many writers as readers, thousands publish regularly with modest recognition. This is one type of success. For still others, success means simply getting published, itself no mean accomplishment. And for the fortunate few with the inner fortitude to achieve it, success means accomplishing what they set out to do, period.

Most of us, however, have introjected the image of the Famous Writer as a criterion of success. This standard inevitably becomes a powerful weapon against recalcitrant creativity: "Get busy this minute so I can be famous!" Such an undigested lump of ambition must be dealt with if we are to mature as writers and as persons. It cannot simply be re-

pressed, the approach of those who profess to "care nothing" about fame (don't believe them!); nor can it be cravenly given in to, either by hero worship or by envy of the celebrated few.

Envy is usually the frog skin concealing the prince of unrealized potential. Envy allows us to duck the responsibility for our own uncultivated worth or talent and project these qualities onto others. The best antidote for envy is thus to convert it into fuel for real-world efforts to advance a career. Feeling envious takes energy. Use that energy in perfecting your own work and actively putting it forward, and a negative emotion becomes a positive act of self-realization.

Understanding the mechanisms of fame is also useful in the process of integrating the "success" shibboleth into your own value system. By understanding, I do not mean sour-grapes rationalizing that dismisses all famous writers as sell-outs; such easy put-downs are only one more expression of envy. More to the point is understanding the social, cultural, and especially the economic forces underlying the publishing business.

In Pakistan, for instance, literature has a higher status than in market-oriented technocracies such as the United States. At readings, audiences recite along with the poet, hissing their appreciation at the end of favorite lines. Western Europe puts a different cultural value on literature than does Central or Eastern Europe, Latin cultures differ from the Far East, British Commonwealth countries have different expectations than Britain herself. The peculiarly American status of literature, in short, is hardly a universal norm. Given this circumstance, the reception of a given work of literature in a given cultural environment always represents a relative, not an absolute, assessment of its worth. (There are no absolute assessments of literary worth.)

Literature is not a discrete entity to be measured by a single aesthetic or commercial yardstick but a conglomera-

tion of trends, fads, and biases with schools and subschools. Most American writers find it strange to describe their work, not in terms of content, but in terms of type, style, and school. To literateurs of other cultures, however, such ignorance of one's formal biases would be grotesque. American writers tend to assume that realism, for instance, is a kind of universal literary lingua franca instead of the recent and stylized development it decidedly is. They are often equally blind to trends in world literature as well as in literary criticism, a field that, in cultures such as France, has a direct and immediate impact on literary styles.

Acquiring literary sophistication can give you something resembling a knowledgeable vantage point from which to view your work's reception in the world. For, apart from its literary merit—which you, its proud parent, will *never* be able to judge objectively—your work is going to be received within a specific cultural framework of unspoken literary assumptions determined by powerful social and intellectual biases. A multicultural and historical perspective, which so few writers trouble to acquire, can not only help you disidentify with your own work's critical reception (as discussed in Chapter 5), it can also make you skeptical of success determined by chance trend and cheerfully (well, *almost* cheerfully) unfazed by crushing failure.

With this extended caveat, let's now turn to the blocks that success, its presence or absence, can generate in the writer.

FEAR OF SUCCESS

Oddly enough, fear of success occurs as much in those who are far from achieving recognition as in those who are close to crossing the threshold. In fact, some writers remain obscure because unconsciously they cannot or do not wish to

experience what they imagine "success" will bring. As a rule, however, the block rises only when public recognition looms threateningly close on the horizon. Suppose you have only one more story to write and a publisher will bring out your collection. Stage fright, a kind of cosmic reluctance, seizes you and you find yourself utterly unable to complete this story—or even begin it. Later, the contract canceled, you indulge in the "sweet lemon" rationalization that your artistic integrity kept you from hacking out a piece just for the craven pleasure of being published. Underneath, however, lurks the nagging, unconfronted truth: *You did not want the book to be published.* Why?

There are likely to be two distinctly separate possible answers, and it takes more honesty than anyone should reasonably be expected to have to determine which is right. The first is that you have sabotaged your chances out of an inner and unacknowledged sense of unworthiness—the demon of self-hatred at work again. But if you come to this bleak conclusion about your own motives, beware the temptation to create a closed circuit of self-blame in which you may now despise yourself for having spoiled your own chances—a double whammy!

The second possible reason for backing away from success is an unconscious conviction that you were not ready for national (or even public) exposure. Why weren't you ready? Again, many hypotheses may be worth considering. A lingering *puer* hesitation to cross the threshold into "actuality" may have affected you. Lack of publication, after all, represents a kind of incompletion or limitlessness; a work becomes truly *real* when it is in print and has an audience. Or, on the other hand, you may have been secretly convinced that your work, and possibly yourself as well, was not ready for the roller coaster ride.

If you are able to suspend punishing self-judgment and

consider any of the multitude of *positive* unconscious reasons you may have had for stumbling on the threshold of success, you are in an excellent position to rectify the situation. If it's *puer* hesitation, perhaps you require more extensive local exposure to prepare yourself emotionally for the big time. You can take steps to get this exposure and start building the foundation for a more solid, gradually achieved success. If your block came from genuine doubts about the value of your work, can you fix it? Or can you sit down now and write something better? A gentle, nonblaming assessment of the situation is most likely to produce good results—instead of years of paralysis. The missed opportunity, in fact, can be gained opportunity if you exploit it as an occasion to learn about your limitations and fears and work positively to grow through them.

Finally, if you are a very young writer who has backed off unconsciously from impending success, you may have done yourself an enormous favor. Literary history is full of stories of those whose unformed personhood was tragically, even fatally, distorted by early success, and your unconscious may have had an inkling that this could have happened to you. The sensible message of the block (which may be a shrewder indicator of your personal strength than you realize), as we say in Chapter 11, is simply this: Cultivate your still-developing art in relative privacy until you have gained enough maturity to assume the responsibilities of public exposure (and possibly success).

ACHIEVING SUCCESS

What happens when you actually do grab the brass ring?

Success provides the writer with expanded opportunities and equally expanded pitfalls. On one hand, it offers a wider audience, financial rewards that allow more time to

write, and a gratifying endorsement of the years of solitary struggle and effort it took you to get this far. Success imparts that incomparably fine feeling of flowing *with* the current after years of ceaseless struggle upstream against indifference and rejection. And the impetus and validation that success provides can spur you to much greater efforts than you might otherwise have attempted.

But success can also open the door to trouble when a writer identifies with fame instead of finding her own center. It can leave her open to inner feelings of guilt and unworthiness, to stage fright at the prospect of letting down an enormously larger audience, or to the harsh criticism from others that comes with being a visible target. A writer who has become not merely successful but famous may succumb to the temptation of making Fame itself a new career, with writing a secondary concern. In the United States especially, literary achievement tends to be confused with celebrity status and personal charisma. Fame on these terms, the *People* magazine variety, is based on a cult of personality that needs to create easily recognizable star personae. This kind of fame represents the ultimate self-fulfillment and self-punishment of narcissism because it crystallizes—and traps—an image of the writer as a personality who supplants his own works as the primary focus of interest. (See, for example, John Raeburn's excellent study of Ernest Hemingway, *Fame Became of Him*, published by Indiana University Press.)

Again we can turn to Norman Mailer for a perceptive insight into the dilemma of such a writer:

> For anyone who's become an author early and has a good deal of success . . . it's not automatic or easy afterwards to look upon other people with a simple interest because generally speaking they're more interested in us than we are in them. . . . it has an immense impact when you're young.

You become a mirror and the only way you can perceive events is through the mirror of your self.

Early success and fame can effectively stunt a young writer's further development. Hemingway and Fitzgerald—and all the others who didn't have a chance to grow up in private—later experienced major blocks. The writer rebels unconsciously against the expectations of the public. A block in this context may have the same symbolic connotation for writers as the weight problem of certain movie stars, who, one suspects, get fat as an unconscious but thoroughly healthy rebellion against the awesome burden of the sexual projections of millions of other humans. (The word "fame" itself derives from the Latin *fama,* meaning rumor or ill report—as if fame inevitably carries the combined worship and resentment of thousands of individual psyches projected onto one of their number.)

To make matters worse, there is a striking lack of correlation between success and literary worth. Success has an almost random quality that makes it especially hard for the individual writer to come to terms with. You never know for sure whether the rewards of success are deserved or undeserved, except as they resonate with your own sense of what is right. If what Rilke called your inner conscience has been twisted beyond recognition between the twin poles of inferiority and inflation, you will be the public's puppet, relying on them to tell you what's right or wrong with your work instead of yourself. The minute you hand over your creative tiller to the world at large, however, you are likely to experience a tremendous block. You have become partners with your public instead of with your creative child, and he/she doesn't like that one bit.

Success gained primarily by manipulation of the literary environment carries no inner resonance and may leave its

recipient in a state of permanent hidden unease which may also eventually be detected by readers, as Cyril Connolly notes with his usual perception:

> The advertising, publicity and enthusiasm which a book generates—in a word its success—imply a reaction against it. The element of inflation in a writer's success, the extent to which it has been forced, is something that has to be written off. One can fool the public about a book but the public will store up resentment in proportion to its folly.

And, Connolly adds ominously, "The public can be fooled deliberately, by advertising and publicity, or it can be fooled by accident, by the writer fooling himself."

Among financially successful writers there is also a "too much free time" malaise. The nemesis of the classic *puer* can strike even the serious producing writer who, after years of scrambling to make ends meet, becomes financially secure, even wealthy, from writing. This new freedom can have the effect of making its recipient feel as shiftless as a teenager, creating an atmosphere of paralysis. A long-standing writing routine can collapse (and has collapsed, many times) after the "petty" demands of earning a daily living are removed.

Writing, as Hemingway once admitted, is not a full-time occupation. You have to do something with the rest of your time, and this is where the marlin fishing—or much worse—begins. As a rule, this paralysis doesn't strike the confirmed "pros," the commercial hacks, but the sensitive writers whose talents are still emerging. It is just this condition of external plenty and internal famine that John Steinbeck may have been describing when, famous at last, he lamented: "The perfect pointed pencil—the paper persuasive—the fantastic chair and a good light and no writing."

Many writers find themselves completely blocked by this removal of mundane pressures, the anticipated heaven turning out to be hell instead. It is as if you had been granted lifetime tenure at the Mawnaweetok Writer's Colony and began slowly to realize that you didn't much relish the prospect. You experience the dread limitlessness of having "all the time in the world" to write, fertile breeding ground for guilt when your creative child rebels at the prospect of writing all the time.

Many books are written out of the spiritual limbo that comes with this complicated adjustment to success. But they are frozen, dead, lifeless works, produced by forcing the block just because you feel that, as an Author, you *ought* to be writing even if your inner creative mechanisms have not wholly adjusted to the new environment of success. Finding your center again after being swept into this maelstrom is no easy thing to do.

NOT ACHIEVING SUCCESS

What of the other (and far more common) side of the success coin? What if you have struggled for years and years with only modest returns for your efforts? What if you have never been allowed to experience that marvelous feeling of being buoyed by public esteem? You feel helpless and frustrated; the nagging voice inside tells you that the public's indifference to you—as to any number of worthless writers—is deadly accurate: You deserve to be unknown because you're no good.

Since success is often, as we have seen, measured on an impossibly high and antiliterary yardstick, it is obvious that each writer is required to formulate an individual standard of success more in keeping with reality.

But lack of success *can* have detrimental effects. Recognition is worthwhile and important; not getting it can make you suffer as a writer. So many creative individuals have suffered undeservedly that popular wisdom tends to be a bit blasé about this circumstance and say it is the "artist's lot." For the truly gifted, however, lack of recognition is an unnatural and unfair state of affairs that benefits neither the writer nor his potential public. Randall Jarrell, in discussing the career of the novelist Christina Stead after the critical failure of her magnificent *The Man Who Loved Children,* had this to say:

> When the world rejects, and then forgets, a writer's most profound and imaginative book, he may unconsciously work in a more limited way in the books that follow it; this has happened, I believe, to Christina Stead. The world's incomprehension has robbed it, for twenty-five years, of *The Man Who Loved Children;* has robbed it, forever, of what could have come after *The Man Who Loved Children.*

The failure to achieve deserved success, however—critical recognition or even publication—can also cause an actual block. You think: Why sit down and write yet another novel/story/poem to be sent out fifty times with no results? Why bring it into the world at all if no one will read it? These are gut feelings that deserve to be taken seriously. Your decision to continue as a writer must be, as always, an individual one. Some experience relief in laying down their pens after years of frustration; others do not.

If you decide to continue writing, some process has probably occurred within you that has consciously or unconsciously adapted you, or resigned you, to an "invisible" career. Your obscurity may be warranted or it may not, but you continue to function as a writer. What is often forgotten, however, is that the vast majority of writers live out their literary lives in just such a penumbra. Only a handful stand in

the sun, and even those have put in a ten- or twenty-year apprenticeship in the shadows.

Moreover, this environment of benign neglect can exert a healthy influence on your work, healthier than the glare of publicity and the review machinery of national publication. Most writers experience an extremely long formative period (if not their entire creative lifetimes) during which they are extremely suggestible. As an unknown, you are free to develop and strengthen your creative identity during this important time; the tentative whisper of your creative child is not being drowned out by the loud, authoritarian voice of critical opinion. Or if obscurity returns after an initial flurry of recognition, you have the rare opportunity to understand just how fickle and irrational the climate of critical opinion can be. It is an opportunity that allows you to *become exactly what you are,* an opportunity those riding the crest of trend and fashion never get. Cloned with public opinion, they are likely to become its prisoners instead.

This is not to belittle those obvious talents who succeed, and deservedly, regardless of the current fashion. But even favored writers often end up having their wrists slapped for failure to conform to the prevailing literary sensibility. Here, only the strength of the inner attitude will save you from going under. Writers such as Jean Rhys, for example, not "discovered" until very old age—when their writing careers are virtually over—may often sound bitter on the surface, but underneath lies the luminous core of understanding that has sustained them:

> All of writing is a huge lake. There are great rivers that feed the lake, like Tolstoi and Dostoevski. And there are trickles, like Jean Rhys. All that matters is feeding the lake. I don't matter. The lake matters. You must keep feeding the lake.

Rhys's attitude vividly illustrates the differences between

what might be called the "ensemble" or repertory view of literature, equally supportive of lead, second-string, and bit players, and the star system, which eats its prey alive. The ensemble ethic supports not just the individual writer but the tradition he carries as well. We, as writers, are bearers of a culture, a language, and a tradition—a fact we often brush aside in our egotistic quest for personal acclaim.

For just this reason I have deliberately avoided a roll call of great writers who were neglected in their lifetimes. What has, say, Melville's example or any one of a hundred such stories to do with most writers? There is no such thing as a model literary career, either for success or for obscurity. None of us is a Melville or Van Gogh; each of us has an individual destiny as a person and as a writer. And the one is no less important than the other. Whether your books are out of print or best-sellers—as the saying goes—they won't cry at your wake.

I SHOULD HAVE BEEN FAMOUS BY NOW
Choose the eminent writer, living or dead, you most admire and compose a dialogue on fame between that person and yourself.

JOYCE, SHAKESPEARE, GOETHE:

YOU:

You may be surprised at the unexpected twists this conversation can take, including the revelation of previously unsuspected values and attitudes you may hold regarding artistic success and recognition.

ACTIVE SILENCE: No Block at All

*Life leads the thoughtful man on a path of many wind-
ings.*
Now the course is checked, now it runs straight again.
Here winged thoughts may pour freely forth in words.
*There the heavy burden of knowledge must be shut
away in silence.*

I Ching, Hexagram 13

Who then . . . tells a finer tale than any of us?
Silence does.

—Isak Dinesen

A variety of silences, unscheduled and unexplained, are likely to fall in every writer's career. This book has examined an array of silences geared to fend off the unreasonable demands of a psyche in disequilibrium. But even in a writer, silence is not always, or even mostly, bad. Silence is often as blessed a condition as its opposite. Writing/not writing represents a natural alternation of states that is individually determined; to steal a metaphor from Coleridge, they are the systole and diastole of the creative life. For every writer who is a systematic worker, another is "erratic." For every writer who allows a month between works, another allows a year.

Some silences in your writing life may be inherently negative (i.e., you fall silent when it may be your moral duty to speak up), but most are likely to be natural occurrences. The silence merely *is*, but you are being negative in refusing its right to existence.

Many kinds of silences happen to writers: thwarted unhappy silences of the kind recorded by Tillie Olsen in her book of the same name; beautiful, restful silences; the stifled silence resulting from censorship; the profound silence of emotional grief; the fertile silence of creative incubation. All these silences represent central experiences of the creative life; all, even the most patently negative, contain the possibility of instructing and enlightening in various profound ways.

Let's examine a few more silences.

THE SILENCE OF INCUBATION

It must be admitted: Sometimes your creative child is silent

for no reason at all. You know he's silent because nothing is coming through to you from the unconscious. But does this silence mean he is inactive? Not necessarily. What about Keats's "delicious diligent indolence," the silence that falls while development continues in unseen ways in your unconscious? "Well," replies the controlling personality, "that story about 'letting the field lie fallow' is the world's hoariest excuse for laziness. Nothing's happening down there—I know because I don't *feel* anything happening. I'm just stalling again."

We know already that the key words "laziness" and "stalling" (read: procrastination) are the buzzwords of an autocratic, punishing consciousness. You are unaware that anything is happening because your unconscious is shielding its sprouting seeds from the harsh glare of your judgmental ego. You will not be allowed in the garden until the plants are tall enough and tough enough to withstand your hobnailed boots. Then, and only then, will you possibly be granted entry.

If you belong to this category of overly impatient writers, it is vital that you consciously adopt a positive, accepting attitude toward your own silence. Patience, acceptance, and trust are the virtues your consciousness must cultivate while your unconscious is active in that other room, behind the closed door. The psychiatrist Rollo May has given a precise description of this state of conscious inactivity coupled with unconscious activity:

[A]n artist's "waiting," funny as it may look in cartoons, is not be to be confused with laziness or passivity. It requires a high degree of attention, as when a diver is poised on the end of the springboard, not jumping but holding his or her muscles in sensitive balance for the right second. It is an active listening, keyed to hear the answer, alert to see whatever can be glimpsed when the vision or the words do come. It is a

waiting for the birthing process to begin to move in its own organic time. It is necessary that the artist have this sense of timing, that he or she respect these periods of receptivity as part of the mystery of creativity and creation.

The more you persist in developing your skills of active waiting, the stronger the bond of trust become between your conscious ego and that mysterious entity on the other side, your creative child. As an added benefit, the intervals of silence may even decrease in proportion to your unquestioning respect for them.

THE SILENCE OF GRIEF

Another silence that commands obedience is the silence of emotional grief as it works through to resolution in the deeper strata of your psyche. Whereas some writers find the act of writing itself a cathartic release after a scarcely bearable life episode, others retreat into merciful silence.

Though the circumstances may be tragic, such a silence is also positive; mourning is an active condition not to be confused with the "hiding from feelings" discussed in Chapter 11. At such times, the full energies of your unconscious may be taken up in the knitting and healing process, leaving nothing left over for creative endeavor. Surrendering yourself to this unseen, sometimes even unfelt, process requires simple blind faith that progress is somehow being made.

An interesting case of a writer who tried and failed to find direct release from grief through his work is that of the poet Stéphane Mallarmé, who planned a literary memorial to his son Anatole, dead at the age of eight. The notes he left for this ambitious work, never completed, reveal an intention to cheat death of its victory by immortalizing the deceased through art. As the critic Leo Bersani acutely commented,

however, "Mallarmé's failure to complete the Anatole epic is perhaps the sign of a reluctance to reduce life to the trivializing nobility of redemption through art." Mallarmé's block may well have represented the victory of his own humanity over an artist's narcissism.

This example is an important reminder that art is not necessarily superior to life; it cannot be vulgarly employed in an effort to cancel out the real losses life imposes on us. When grief provides a channel for creative expression, the writer can permissibly follow his natural tendencies. When it closes down the unconscious, the writer must accept this outcome, too.

RANDOM SILENCES

Again and again, the invisibility or inaccessibility of unconscious processes tempts us to worry over all our silences. Because the conscious self receives no messages, it assumes the unconscious is doing nothing. When you find yourself not quite trusting a silence, examine yourself first for signs of the various psychological dysfunctions described in earlier chapters. If none of them seems to be the motive, you must be prepared to accept and acknowledge your "block" as an unidentifiable active silence. Give your creative child some credit. You may never know exactly why it has drawn back from you, but you must respect its wish to do so.

A seemingly gratuitous silence imposed on the ego is part of the inherent irrationality of life. It is galling, after all, that we are never smart enough, clear-sighted enough, or prescient enough to see the full scope of our lives at any given moment, or their future direction. Artists especially, concerned as they are to bring order and meaning out of chaos, can find this a hard pill to swallow. Artists of all types are reluctant to accept that the source and continuity of their art is

rooted in "meaninglessness"—that is, something outside their conscious control.

The gulf between intent and execution, for example, remains highly mysterious and unpredictable for many writers. Few would fail to recognize the state Jean Cocteau described when he lamented that it never seemed possible to "do what one *intends*":

> I feel myself inhabited by a force or being—very little known to me. It gives the orders; I follow. The conception of my novel *Les Enfants Terribles* came to me from a friend. . . . I commenced to write: exactly seventeen pages per day. It went well. I was pleased with it. Very. There was in the original life story some connection with America, and I had something I wanted to say about America. Poof! The being in me did not want to write that! Dead halt. A month of stupid staring at paper unable to say anything. One day it commenced again in its own way.
>
> . . . When you speak of these things to one who works systematically . . . they think you jest. Or that you are lazy and use this as an excuse. Put yourself at a desk and write! You are a writer, are you not? *Violà!* I have tried this. What comes is no good. *Never any good.* Claudel at his desk from nine to twelve. It is unthinkable to work like that!

And what of Samuel Taylor Coleridge, our favorite whipping boy, master of the slippery excuse and blocked writer par excellence? Earlier we quoted Cyril Connolly praising Coleridge's silence, and here, E. M. Forster's matching epitaph:

> He seldom did what he or what others hoped, and posterity has marked him as her prey in consequence. She had never ceased to hold up her plump finger to him, and shake it and say that he has disappointed her. . . . But if one turns on

posterity and says, "Well! what else do you want him to do? Would you rather have [Coleridge] as he is or not at all?" she is apt to be silent or to change the conversation.

As with Connolly, more than disinterested championing of an author may have been at work here, as Forster's own fictional output was relatively small, a fact that prompted Elizabeth Bowen to comment:

> Mr. Forster's intervals of silence have been a perplexity, as well as a deprivation. Silences, in a man from whom we have exorbitant expectations, take on a sort of positive character.

Ultimately, the extended silences of such writers carries tremendous resonance, for the collective anticipation of their audience gives their few works special intensity of impact.

Blaming oneself for low productivity, in short, is punishment for a crime that did not exist until it was named. An uneven artistic output is a natural condition of creativity for many.

THE LAST WORD

The day you find out you're a writer is usually not the day you finish your first story or poem or the day you are first published, but much, much later. It is the day you realize you possess a certain cluster of traits that forms the writing obsession. Far from feeling crowned by laurel, you are likely to experience a reaction akin to hearing, on your twenty-first birthday, that you are descended from a venerable line of Transylvanian vampires and that you are one, too; there is no escape! For by this time, you have probably had ample opportunity to observe, in yourself as well as in other writers, some of the psychological stigmata of the creative person: hypersensitivity, self-absorption, devouring ambition, and

all those related traits that tend to cancel out the romantic aura the profession holds in the eyes of the uninitiated.

Before severe depression sets in, however, here is a simple distinction between neurosis and art. It is *not* neurotic to sit at a desk all day devising an imaginary world. It is not even neurotic to sit all day at a desk trying to devise an imaginary world but not succeeding in doing so.

What *is* neurotic is to hate yourself for doing/not doing either of these activities. Let Otto Rank speak to the point:

> The neurotic, no matter whether productive or obstructed, suffers fundamentally from the fact that he cannot or will not accept himself, his own individuality, his own personality. On one hand he criticizes himself to excess, which means that he makes too great demands on himself and his completeness, so that failing to attain leads only to more self-criticism. If we take this thwarted type . . . and compare him to the artist, it is at once clear that the artist is in a sense the antithesis to the self-critical neurotic type. Not that the artist does not criticize himself, but by accepting his personality he not only fulfills that for which the neurotic is striving in vain but goes far beyond it. The precondition, then, of the creative personality is not only its acceptance but its actual glorification of itself.

Viewed in Rank's benign perspective, the *frissons* of egotism and other eccentricities often found in the creative personality are, like a mild dose of asbestos poisoning, occupational hazards—nothing terminal.

For our purposes, however, Rank has identified the most important silence available to the creative person—namely, the active verb *to silence*. For a writer, this is truly the "last word." In silencing the voice of relentless self-hatred, the writer gains in fulfilled humanity as well as art. The consequences of that triumphant silencing, if renewed daily, will echo for a lifetime.

APPENDIX

THE PERSON FROM PORLOCK:
A PORTFOLIO
When the poem "Kubla Khan" was published in 1816, Samuel Taylor Coleridge appended the following explanation of its fragmentary nature. The ever-so-slightly suspect plausibility of the statement has created a lingering ripple in English literary history, as suggested by the two poetical responses by the twentieth-century poets Robert Graves and Stevie Smith.*

In the summer of the year 1797, the Author, then in ill health, had retired to a lonely farm-house between Porlock and Linton, on the Exmoor confines of Somerset and Devonshire. In consequence of a slight indisposition, an anodyne had been prescribed, from the effects of which he fell asleep in his chair at the moment that he was reading the following sentence, or words of the same substance, in "Purchas's Pilgrimage": "Here the Khan Kubla commanded a palace to be built, and a stately garden thereunto. And thus ten miles of fertile ground were inclosed with a wall." The Author continued for about three hours in a profound sleep, at least of the external senses, during which time he has the most vivid con-

*Vladimir Nabokov's working title for his novel *Bend Sinister* was "Person from Porlock." In this choice, Nabokov aficionados will recognize the master's delight in weaving authorial self-consciousness into the fabric of his art.

fidence, that he could not have composed less than from two to three hundred lines; if that indeed can be called composition in which all the images rose up before him as *things*, with a parallel production of the correspondent expressions, without any sensation or consciousness of effort. On awaking he appeared to himself to have a distinct recollection of the whole, and taking his pen, ink, and paper, instantly and eagerly wrote down the lines that are here preserved. At this moment he was unfortunately called out by a person on business from Porlock, and detained by him above an hour, and on his return to his room, found, to his no small surprise and mortification, that though he still retained some vague and dim recollection of the general purport of the vision, yet, with the exception of some eight or ten scattered lines and images, all the rest had passed away like the images on the surface of a stream into which a stone has been cast, but, alas! without the after restoration of the latter!

THE PERSON FROM PORLOCK

Unkind fate sent the Porlock person
To collect fivepence from a poet's house;
Pocketing which old debt he drove away,
Heedless and gay, homeward bound for Porlock.

O Porlock person, habitual scapegoat,
Should any masterpiece be marred or scotched,
I wish your burly fist on the front door
Had banged yet oftener in literature!
                                            —Robert Graves

THOUGHTS ABOUT THE PERSON
FROM PORLOCK

Coleridge received the Person from Porlock
And ever after called him a curse,
Then why did he hurry to let him in?
He could have hid in the house.

It was not right of Coleridge in fact it was wrong
(But often we all do wrong)
As the truth is I think he was already stuck
With Kubla Khan.

He was weeping and wailing: I am finished, finished,
I shall never write another word of it,
When along comes the Person from Porlock
And takes the blame for it.

I was not right, it was wrong,
But often we all do wrong.

May we inquire the name of the Person from Porlock?
Why, Porson, didn't you know?
He lived at the bottom of Porlock Hill
So had a long way to go,

He wasn't much in the social sense
Though his grandmother was a Warlock,
One of the Rutlandshire ones I fancy
And nothing to do with Porlock,

And he lived at the bottom of the hill as I said
And had a cat named Flo,
And had a cat named Flo.

I long for the Person from Porlock
To bring my thoughts to an end,
I am becoming impatient to see him
I think of him as a friend,

Often I look out of the window
Often I run to the gate
I think, He will come this evening,
I think it is rather late.

I am hungry to be interrupted
For ever and ever amen
O Person from Porlock come quickly
And bring my thoughts to an end.

I felicitate the people who have a Person from Porlock
To break up everything and throw it away
Because then there will be nothing to keep them
And they need not stay.

Why do they grumble so much?
He comes like a benison
They should be glad he has not forgotten them
They might have had to go on.

These thoughts are depressing I know. They are
    depressing
I wish I was more cheerful, it is more pleasant,
Also it is a duty, we should smile as well as submitting
To the purpose of One Above who is experimenting
With various mixtures of human character which goes
    best
All is interesting for him it is exciting, but not for us.
There I go again. Smile, smile, and get some work to
    do
Then you will be practically unconscious without
    positively having to go.

—Stevie Smith

NOTES

Frontispiece quote from *The Diaries of Franz Kafka 1910-1913*, ed. Max Brod (New York: Schocken Books, 1965), p. 264.

Chapter 1

4   Jean Cocteau, interview, *Writers at Work: The Paris Review Interviews*, 3rd ser., ed. George Plimpton (New York: Penguin Books, 1978), p. 67.

5   Tillie Olsen, *Silences* (New York: Delacorte Press/Seymour Lawrence, 1978), p. 6; George Eliot, *Middlemarch* (New York: Harcourt, Brace & World, 1962), p.275. An excellent discussion of the origin of the term "writer's block" and its progress in literary history may be found in the first book-length scholarly work on the subject, *Writer's Block*, by Zachary Leader, to be published by Johns Hopkins Press in 1986.

7   Gerard Manley Hopkins, Poem 69, *The Poems of Gerard Manley Hopkins*, 4th ed. (London: Oxford University Press, 1967).

Chapter 2

14   Richard Wilhelm and Cary F. Baynes, *I Ching* (Princeton, N.J.: Princeton University Press, 1971), p. 16.

17   William Stafford, *Writing the Australian Crawl*, quoted in *The Writer*, February 1982, p. 17.

17   Philip Roth, *The Ghost Writer* (New York: Farrar, Straus & Giroux, 1979), pp. 17-18.

20   Tillie Olsen, *Silences* (New York: Delacorte Press/Seymour Lawrence, 1978), p. 38.

26   Fritz Perls, *Gestalt Therapy Verbatim*, ed. John O. Stevens (New York: Bantam Books, 1972), p. 22.

Chapter 3

34   Samuel Taylor Coleridge, letter quoted in *Poetical Works of S. T. Coleridge*, ed. James Dykes Campbell (London: Macmillan & Co., 1938), p. lv.

37   Stanislaw Jerzy Lec, *Alle Unfrisierte Gedanken [Uncombed Thoughts]*, ed. Karl Dedecius (Munich: Carl Hauser, 1982), p. 66.

Chapter 4

43   Fritz Perls, *Gestalt Therapy Verbatim*, ed. John O. Stevens (New York: Bantam Books, 1971), pp. 20-21.

44   Machen, Arthur

46   *The Journal of Eugène Delacroix*, trans. Walter Pach (New York: Crown Publishers, 1948), p. 89.

47   Perls, *Gestalt Therapy*, p. 19.

50   Muriel Schiffman, *Gestalt Self Therapy* (Menlo Park, Calif.: Self Therapy Press, 1971), p. 63.

52   Donald Newlove, *Those Drinking Days: Myself and Other Writers* (New York: Horizon Press, 1981), pp. 100-102.

54   Christopher Isherwood, interview, *Writers at Work: The Paris Review Interviews*, 4th ser., ed. George Plimpton (New York: Penguin Books, 1976), p. 219.

Chapter 5

58   Robert Graves, interview, *Writers at Work: The Paris Review Interviews*, 4th ser., ed. George Plimpton (New York: Penguin Books, 1976), p. 65.

60   William Searle, editorial, *Occident*, Fall 1963, p. 4.

62   Cyril Connolly, *Enemies of Promise* (New York: Macmillan, 1948), p. 87.

65   Evelyn Waugh, "Urbane Enjoyment Personified: Sir Osbert Sitwell," in *A Little Order*, ed. Donat Gallagher (Boston: Little, Brown & Co., 1977), p. 97.

67   Cynthia Ozick, quoted in "A Writer's First Readers," by Helen Benedict, *New York Times Book Review*, February 6, 1983, p. 11.

69   Diane Wakoski, interview, "Conversation with Diane Wakoski," *Hawaii Review*, Fall 1979, p. 27.

Chapter 6

72   John Leggett, *Ross and Tom: Two American Tragedies* (New York: Simon & Schuster, 1974), p. 116.

74   Katherine Mansfield, *The Letters and Journals: A Selection*, ed. C. K. Stead (Middlesex: Penguin Books, 1977), p. 234.

75   Quoted in Aileen Ward, *John Keats: The Making of a Poet* (New York: Viking Press, 1963), p. 84.

76   Sir Humphry Davy, about Coleridge, quoted in *Poetical Works of S. T. Coleridge*, ed. James Dykes Campbell (London: Macmillan & Co., 1938).

77   James Joyce, *A Portrait of the Artist as a Young Man* (New York: Viking Press, 1956), p. 253.

77   The phrase is Donald Newlove's. *Those Drinking Days: Myself and Other Writers* (New York: Horizon Press, 1981), p. 138.

78   Anaïs Nin, *Diaries: 1934-1939*, ed. Gunther Stuhlmann, vol. 2 (New York: Harcourt, Brace & World, 1967), p. 20.

78   Lawrence Durrell, quoted in *Time*, "Beating Writer's Block," October 31, 1977, p. 101.

78   Lec, *Uncombed Thoughts*.

80   Newlove, *Those Drinking Days*, pp. 125, 126.

80   Cyril Connolly, *Enemies of Promise* (New York: Macmillan, 1948), p. 106.

81   Delmore Schwartz, quoted in James Atlas, *Delmore Schwartz: The Life of an American Poet* (New York: Avon Books, 1978), p. 175.

81   Charles Jackson, *The Lost Weekend* (New York: Noonday Press, 1960), p. 46.

82   Newlove, *Those Drinking Days*, p. 125.

82   Charles Lamb, "Sanity of True Genius," *Complete Works and Letters* (New York: Random House, 1935), p. 167.

84   Ward, *John Keats*, pp. 260-61.

Chapter 7

87   Wendell Berry, "Poetry and Marriage," in *Standing by Words* (San Francisco: North Point Press, 1983), p. 204.

88   Milan Kundera, *Book of Laughter and Forgetting* (New York: Penguin Books, 1981), p. 106.

89   Marie Louise von Franz, *Puer Aeternus* (New York: Spring Publications, 1970), p. 2. My discussion of the *puer aeternus* figure is indebted to von Franz's ground-breaking analysis.

90   Robert Musil, *The Man Without Qualities* (London: Pan, 1979), vol. 1, p. 297; vol. 2, p. 33.

91   For this discussion and for information on Hartley Coleridge, I am indebted to Daphne du Maurier's excellent study, *The Infernal World of Branwell Brontë* (New York: Pocket Books, 1962).

Chapter 8

98   George Eliot, *Middlemarch* (New York: Harcourt, Brace & World, 1962), p. 273.

99   See Carobeth Laird, *Encounter with an Angry God* (New York: Ballantine Books, 1977).

100   Frank O'Connor, interview, *Writers at Work: The Paris Review Interviews*, 1st ser., ed. Malcolm Cowley (New York: Penguin Books, 1958), p. 168.

101   Rollo May, *The Courage to Create* (New York: W. W. Norton & Co., 1975), pp. 69-70.

104   Feodor Dostoevski, letter to A. V. Korvin-Krukovskaya, excerpted in *Crime and Punishment*, trans. Jessie Coulson (rev.), ed. George Gibian (New York: W. W. Norton & Co., 1975), p. 480f.

105   John Steinbeck, *Journal of a Novel: The East of Eden Letters* (New York: Viking Press, 1969), p. 84.

105   Eileen Simpson, *Poets in Their Youth: A Memoir* (New York: Random House, 1982), p. 93.

105   Anne Tyler, quoted in "A Writer's First Readers," by Helen
        Benedict, *New York Times Book Review*, February 6, 1983, p. 24.

106   Anthony Burgess, interview, *Writers at Work: The Paris Review
        Interviews*, 4th ser., ed. George Plimpton (New York: Penguin
        Books, 1977), p. 332.

Chapter 9

110   Jorge Luis Borges, interview, *Writers at Work: The Paris Review
        Interviews*, 4th ser., ed. George Plimpton (New York: Penguin
        Books, 1977), p. 123.

111   Norman Mailer, *Cannibals and Christians* (New York: Dial
        Press, 1966), p. 124.

112   Cyril Connolly, *Enemies of Promise* (New York: Macmillan,
        1948), p. 24.

116   Gore Vidal, "French Letters: Theories of the New Novel," in
        Homage to Daniel Shays: Collected Essays 1952-1972 (New
        York: Vintage Books, 1973), p. 279.

117   S. J. Perelman, interview, *Writers at Work: The Paris Review In-
        terviews*, 2nd ser., ed. George Plimpton (New York: Penguin
        Books, 1982), p. 248.

Chapter 10

120   Edward Albee, interview, *Writers at Work: The Paris Review In-
        terviews*, 3rd ser., ed. George Plimpton (New York: Penguin
        Books, 1977), p. 328.

125   Rainer Maria Rilke, *Letters*, trans. Jane Barnard Greene and M.
        D. Herter Norton, vol. 1 (New York: W. W. Norton & Co., 1947-
        48), p. 319.

126   Jorge Luis Borges, interview, *Writers at Work: The Paris Review
        Interviews*, 4th ser., ed. George Plimpton (New York: Penguin
        Books, 1976), p. 123.

127   Rilke, *Letters*, vol. 1, p. 318.

128   Tom Wolfe, *The Kandy-Colored Tangerine-Flake Streamline Ba-
        by* (New York: Farrar, Straus & Giroux, 1965), pp. ix-xii.

Chapter 11

134   Edna St. Vincent Millay, "Renascence," *Collected Poems* (New York: Harper & Row, 1956).

137   John Stuart Mill, *Autobiography* (New York: Columbia University Press, 1960), p. 97.

137   Milan Kundera, *Life Is Elsewhere*, trans. Peter Kussi (New York: Alfred A. Knopf, 1974), p. 205.

138   Mill, *Autobiography*, p. 93.

138   Elizabeth Bowen, *Collected Impressions* (New York: Alfred A. Knopf, 1950), p. 18.

140   Tadeusz Konwicki, *A Minor Apocalypse*, trans. Richard Lourie (New York: Farrar, Straus & Giroux, 1983), p. 3.

141   *The Diaries of Franz Kafka 1910-1913*, ed. Max Brod (New York: Schocken Books, 1965), p. 33.

141   Louise Bogan, *Journey Around My Room: The Autobiography of Louise Bogan*, ed. Ruth Limmer (New York: Viking Press, 1980), p. 116.

142   Lec, *Uncombed Thoughts*, f.p.

143   Douglas Day, *Malcolm Lowry: A Biography* (New York: Oxford University Press, 1973), p. 72.

144   Cyril Connolly, *Enemies of Promise* (New York: Macmillan Co., 1948), p. 111.

145   Rainer Maria Rilke, *Letters*, trans. Jane Barnard Greene and M. D. Herter Norton, vol. 1 (New York: W. W. Norton & Co., 1947-48), p. 300.

Chapter 12

148   Cyril Connolly, quoted in *Time*, "Beating Writer's Block," October 31, 1977, p. 101.

149   Saul Bellow, interview, *Writers at Work: The Paris Review Interviews*, 3rd ser., ed. George Plimpton (New York: Penguin Books, 1975), p. 186.

154   Norman Mailer, quoted in "Mailer Talking," by Michiko Kakutani, *New York Times Book Review*, June 6, 1982, p. 3.

156   Cyril Connolly, *Enemies of Promise* (New York: Macmillan Co., 1948), p. 7.

156   John Steinbeck, *Journal of a Novel: The East of Eden Letters* (New York: Viking Press, 1969), p. 6.

156   Randall Jarrell, Introduction, *The Man Who Loved Children*, by Christina Stead (New York: Holt, Rinehart & Winston, 1965), p. xxxix.

159   Jean Rhys, quoted in David Plante, *Difficult Women: A Memoir of Three* (New York: Atheneum Publishers, 1983), p. 22.

Chapter 13

162   Richard Wilhelm and Cary F. Baynes, *I Ching* (Princeton, N.J.: Princeton University Press, 1971), Hexagram 13, p. 56.

162   Isak Dinesen, "The Blank Page," in *Last Tales* (New York: Random House, 1957), p. 100. Read the story to discover the scandalous significance of the "blank page."

164   John Keats, *Letters*, ed. Robert Gittings (London: Oxford University Press, 1970).

164   Rollo May, *The Courage to Create* (New York: W. W. Norton & Co., 1975), p. 81.

167   Jean Cocteau, interview, *Writers at Work: The Paris Review Interviews*, 3rd ser., ed. George Plimpton (New York: Penguin Books, 1975), pp. 66-69.

168   E. M. Forster, "Trooper Silas Tomkyn Comberbacke," *Abinger Harvest* (New York: Meridian Books, 1955), p. 216.

168   Elizabeth Bowen, *Collected Impressions* (New York: Alfred A. Knopf, 1950), p. 126.

169   Otto Rank, *The Myth of the Birth of the Hero* (New York: Vintage Books, 1959), p. 131.

Appendix

170   Samuel Taylor Coleridge, *Poems*, ed. Ernest Hartley Coleridge (London: Oxford University Press, 1960).

170   See *The Nabokov-Wilson Letters*, ed. Simon Karlinsky (New York: Harper & Row, 1979), pp. 123, 169f.

171   Robert Graves, *Collected Poems* (Garden City, N.Y.: Doubleday & Co., 1961), p. 342.

173   Stevie Smith, *Selected Poems*, ed. James MacGibbon (London: Penguin Books, 1978), pp. 230-32.

INDEX

Other Books of Interest

General Writing Books

Beginning Writer's Answer Book, edited by Kirk Polking $14.95

Getting the Words Right: How to Revise, Edit, and Rewrite, by Theodore A. Rees Cheney $13.95

How to Become a Bestselling Author, by Stan Corwin, $14.95

How to Get Started in Writing, by Peggy Teeters $10.95

How to Write a Book Proposal, by Michael Larsen $9.95

If I Can Write, You Can Write, by Charlie Shedd $12.95

Knowing Where to Look: The Ultimate Guide to Research, by Lois Horowitz $16.95

The 29 Most Common Writing Mistakes & How to Avoid Them, by Judy Delton $9.95

Writer's Block & How to Use It, by Victoria Nelson $12.95

Writer's Encyclopedia, edited by Kirk Polking $19.95

Writer's Market, $19.95

Writer's Resource Guide, edited by Bernadine Clark $16.95

Writing From the Inside Out, by Charlotte Edwards (paper) $9.95

Fiction Writing

Fiction Is Folks: How to Create Unforgettable Characters, by Robert Newton Peck $11.95

Fiction Writer's Market, edited by Jean Fredette $17.95

Handbook of Short Story Writing, edited by Dickson and Smythe (paper) $6.95

Storycrafting, by Paul Darcy Boles $14.95

Writing Romance Fiction—For Love and Money, by Helene Schellenberg Barnhart $14.95

Writing the Novel: From Plot to Print, by Lawrence Block $10.95

Special Interest Writing Books

Complete Book of Scriptwriting, by J. Michael Straczynski $14.95

The Craft of Lyric Writing, by Sheila Davis $16.95

How to Write a Cookbook and Get It Published, by Sara Pitzer, $15.95

How to Write a Play, by Raymond Hull $13.95

How to Write & Sell (Your Sense of) Humor, by Gene Perret $12.95

How to Write the Story of Your Life, by Frank P. Thomas $12.95

On Being a Poet, by Judson Jerome $14.95

Poet's Handbook, by Judson Jerome $11.95

TV Scriptwriter's Handbook, by Alfred Brenner (paper) $9.95

Travel Writer's Handbook, by Louise Zobel (paper) $8.95

Writing for Children & Teenagers, by Lee Wyndham (paper) $9.95

Writing for the Soaps, by Jean Rouverol $14.95

The Writing Business

Complete Guide to Self-Publishing, by Tom & Marilyn Ross $19.95

Complete Handbook for Freelance Writers, by Kay Cassill $14.95

To order directly from the publisher, include $1.50 postage and handling for 1 book and 50¢ for each additional book. Allow 30 days for delivery.

Writer's Digest Books, Dept. B, 9933 Alliance Rd., Cincinnati OH 45242
Prices subject to change without notice.